CONTENTS

HOW TO USE THIS BOOK

This book is divided into two main parts: the AS part ('Narrative and explanation') and the A2 part ('Analysis and interpretation'). The AS part (comprising eight chapters) explains the history of Italy between 1815 and 1871, and is written as a descriptive analysis. It is hoped that all of the themes of the *Risorgimento* are explained in these chapters. The aim here is to give students information they can use to inform their interpretations about the main features of the unification of Italy. The text is complemented with explanations that hope to further a student's understanding of the topic. Although Italy was unified in 1871, it is important to look beyond that date to see how the new state developed. Therefore, the final chapter acts as a postscript to outline what happened to Italy after 1871. Summary questions complete each chapter. These can be answered orally in class, on paper or be set for homework.

The A2 part of the book is divided into six sections, which attempt to analyse some of the main questions about the *Risorgimento* and the process of Italian unification. Certain key themes have been identified, which will hopefully lead students into debate. It is important that the AS part of the book is read before the analytical A2 part, because a certain understanding of events is assumed. The analytical part is not solely for students studying the topic at A2. It is hoped that AS students will read the second part to extend their knowledge and deepen their understanding of the topic. Several themes identified in the AS part are dealt with at another level in the A2 part, and the ideas of many of the leading historians on the topic are introduced.

Assessment sections, which give advice to students taking examinations for any of the three English examination boards, complete both the AS and A2 parts of the book.

Italian Unification 1820–71

Martin Collier

Series Editors
Martin Collier
Rosemary Rees

Heinemann

Heinemann Educational Publishers
Halley Court, Jordan Hill, Oxford, OX2 8EJ
Part of Harcourt Education Limited

Heinemann is the registered trademark of Harcourt Education Limited

First published 2003

ISBN 0 435 32754 2
07 06 05 04 03
10 9 8 7 6 5 4 3 2 1

Designed, illustrated and typeset by Wyvern 21 Ltd

Original illustrations © Harcourt Education Limited 2003

Printed and bound in the UK by Bath Press Ltd

Index compiled by Ian D. Crane

Photographic acknowledgements
The author and publisher would like to thank the following for permission to
reproduce photographs:
AKG: 11, 38, 69, 81
Bridgeman/Museo del Risorgimento, Turin: 112 (left)
Corbis: 45
Corbis/Bettman: 25
Corbis/Hulton: 22, 32, 112 (right)
Mary Evans Picture Library: 64
Moro Roma/Museo Centrale del Risorgimento: 24

Cover photograph: © Corbis. The picture is 'Garibaldi with the Red Shirts in the
Battle of Calatfimi.'

Picture research by Bea Thomas

Dedication
To my Mother and Father.

Tel: 01865 888084 www.heinemann.co.uk

AS SECTION: NARRATIVE AND EXPLANATION

INTRODUCTION

In 1871, Italy was united as a nation state with Rome as its capital. To us this is no surprise. Italy is seen as one of the leading European states today with an unrivalled richness of history and culture. Yet the process of political unification was not inevitable. The roots of national consciousness in Italy go back beyond the years of Napoleonic rule in Italy.

However, awareness of national identity was never widespread. The Italian peninsula in the nineteenth century and beforehand was a patchwork of political states – from Lombardy, Venice and the Kingdom of Sardinia in the north, to the Kingdom of Naples in the South. It was also a patchwork of dialects and customs, ruled by Italian kings and dukes, and foreign powers. In central Italy, the Pope ruled over the Papal States.

From 1798 until 1814, the Italian peninsula was dominated by France and the rule, either direct or indirect, of Napoleon I (Napoleon Bonaparte). Although Napoleonic rule was ended in 1815, and the kings and dukes of the Italian states were restored to their thrones, French rule left its mark. While ruling Italy, the French had introduced administrative reforms, many of which lasted beyond 1815. They also introduced, among certain classes, ideas of individual freedom and liberty.

After 1815, the Italian peninsula was dominated by Austria, which intervened whenever necessary to prevent the spread of revolution – as in 1821 and 1831. Those pushing for political change were not necessarily nationally minded, but wished for reform at a local level.

However, most of the Italian peninsula was wracked by the revolutions of 1848, as was most of Europe.

The *Risorgimento* is the name given to the process that ended with the political unification of Italy in 1871. It was primarily a cultural movement, aimed at spreading awareness of Italian culture and identity. However, there were significant political thinkers of the *Risorgimento* – most noticeably Guiseppe Mazzini. His belief in an Italy united as a democratic state was revolutionary for his time. Others put forward suggestions for a more conservative settlement. Vincenzo Gioberti argued in the 1840s for the creation of an Italian Federation under the leadership of the Pope. Whatever the differences, all were agreed that the Austrians should be expelled from Lombardy and Venice, which they had controlled since 1815.

In 1848 and 1849, attempts were made to expel the Austrians from the Italian peninsula. But these attempts failed and the lesson was learned that foreign military support would be necessary if such an action was to be successful. The following decade saw the emergence of Piedmont as the only Italian state capable of engineering such support.

Under the capable leadership of its prime minister, Count Camillo Cavour, Piedmont became allied with France and, in 1859, fought a partially successful war of liberation. However, the result of an accidental series of events and the intervention of one of the great heroes of the *Risorgimento*, Guiseppe Garibaldi, resulted in the near complete unification of Italy by 1861. Only Venice and Rome remained in foreign or papal hands. Again, circumstance intervened and events outside Italy contrived to result in the full unification of Italy as a nation state by 1871.

This introduction has been highly simplistic, but hopefully it introduces to you some of the key themes of this period of Italian history.

KEY THEMES OF THE AS SECTION

- The impact of Napoleonic rule: how the legacy of French rule in Italy influenced the development of Italy for the next 60 years.
- The *Risorgimento*: the flowering of the cultural movement in the wake of the return of the old rulers to Italy in 1815 gave those who wished to see political unity an idealistic justification for their actions.
- The influence of Austria: from 1848 to 1859, Austria dominated the Italian peninsula politically. Only with the decline in Austrian power and the emergence of France and Prussia was there an increased possibility for political change in Italy.
- Other foreign powers: Prussia, France, Britain and even (indirectly) Russia, had an important part to play in the process of Italian unification.
- The role of individuals: Mazzini, Cavour and Garibaldi were three of a number of individuals who influenced the course of Italian unification and who were most significant in the story that is about to be told.
- The Italian states: the relative strengths of the Italian states, especially after 1848, are critical in explaining why it was Piedmont that emerged as the dominant state.

CHAPTER 1

What was Italy like in 1815?

INTRODUCTION

In September 1870, the troops of the Italian king **Victor Emmanuel II** entered Rome. Italian unification – bringing together different states of the Italian **peninsula** under one government – was complete. The *Risorgimento* – the reawakening of Italy – had reached its climax. However, the creation of the new Italian state was not inevitable; neither had it been planned. Although Italian unification had taken place, there was little enthusiasm for the new state among the Italian people. In 1861, an Italian politician named **Massimo d'Azeglio** remarked to Victor Emmanuel: 'Sir, we have made Italy. Now we must make Italians.' The story of what follows is of how Italy was made, but it is also the story of division and failure.

THE STATES OF THE PENINSULA

Towards the end of the eighteenth century the peninsula of Italy was home to a number of states.

The Kingdom of Sardinia (Piedmont). From its capital city of Turin, the **House of Savoy** ruled this relatively poor part of Italy. Despite its poverty, successive rulers built up a strong army and governed with an effective civil service. The island of Sardinia was particularly backward and was sparsely populated. Until 1815, the important port of Genoa was part of the Republic of Genoa. It was politically separate from the Kingdom of Sardinia.

Lombardy and Venetia. In the 1790s, Lombardy was part of the Austrian Empire. Its capital, Milan, was the second largest city of that empire. Lombardy was ruled by Austrian officials who acted in the name of the Austrian Emperor. However, they were given a fair degree of

The main regions of Italy at the end of the eighteenth century.

SWITZERLAND

AUSTRIA

SAVOY

Como

LOMBARDY

VENETIA

Legnago

ISTRIA

OTTOMAN EMPIRE

Turin

Milan

Verona

Peschiera

Venice

FRANCE

PIEDMONT

Po

Mantua

Liguria

PARMA

MODENA

Bologna

DALMATIA

NICE

Romagna

Monaco

Florence

Ancona

Livorno

TUSCANY

Marche

Adriatic Sea

ELBA

PAPAL STATES

CORSICA

Umbria

Abruzzi

Rome

NAPLES

SARDINIA

Tyrrhenian Sea

Naples

Cagliari

Calabria

Palmero

SICILY

Mediterranean Sea

N

KEY AREAS

Quadrilateral The area dominated by the fortress towns of Legnago, Mantua, Verona and Peschiera.

Po Valley The River Po runs across the northern Italian plain. Fed by water from the Alps, it irrigates the land that surrounds it – making the land very fertile. This made those who farmed the land of the Po Valley wealthy and politically influential.

freedom to act as they saw fit. The Austrian army underpinned imperial rule. It maintained a number of military strongholds known as the **Quadrilateral**, which dominated the plain of the fertile **Po Valley**.

Republic of Venice. Otherwise known as the Republic of St Mark, this had been a powerful state in the fifteenth and sixteenth centuries because its merchants dominated trade in the Mediterranean. By the 1790s, the republic had lost its importance as a trading power, although not its architectural or artistic splendour.

The Central Duchies. This refers to the independent states of Tuscany, Modena and Parma.

- Tuscany had been governed by part of the Habsburg family, the House of Lorraine, since the 1730s. Relatively prosperous, Tuscany had been at the heart of the **Renaissance** from the fourteenth to sixteenth centuries. The city of Florence (the capital of Tuscany) became home to artists such as Leonardo da Vinci and Michelangelo.
- Modena and Parma were separated from Tuscany by the Appenine Mountains. These two states had a certain political independence – although, like Tuscany, they were within the sphere of Austrian influence.

The Kingdom of Naples. Ruled by the Bourbon family, the Kingdom of Naples was the poorest region of Italy. It was dominated by Naples, the largest city in Italy at the end of the eighteenth century with a population of 400,000. However, most of the population of Naples, and indeed the whole of the kingdom, lived in desperate poverty. In the countryside, the social structure and economic system was unchanged from medieval times. The land was owned by a few absentee landlords and the Church. The kings of Naples were absolute rulers who maintained large armies in order to control the people. As late as 1847, the writer Luigi Settembrini wrote of the Kingdom of Naples: 'No state in Europe is in a worse condition than ours … In the country that is said to be the garden of Europe, the people die of hunger and are in a state worse than beasts.'

THE IMPACT OF THE FRENCH REVOLUTION, 1789

The French Revolution of 1789 was to have a profound effect on Europe. Its impact on the development of Italy should not be underestimated. The revolution in France led to:

- the absolute monarchy being swept away, and
- the introduction of political and administrative reform – based, at least in theory, on the idea of liberty.

Such ideas frightened the rulers of much of the rest of Europe. In 1792, Prussia and Austria launched into war on revolutionary France. This affected Italy because of the (see Key Term on page 45).

KEY PERSON

Napoleon Bonaparte (1769–1821), Napoleon I Emperor of France from 1804–14 and again in 1815. A brilliant general, he also introduced a number of administrative reforms in France that have lasted until today.

KEY AREA

Papal States Stretching from the cities of Ferrara and Bologna in the north down to Benevento in the south, the Papal States dominated central Italy. They were ruled by the head of the Catholic Church, who resided in Rome (for centuries the centre of the Catholic world). The Pope was not just a spiritual leader, he also had temporal power (see Key Term on page 45). To most Popes, control of the Papal States was considered essential to the protection of papal independence. However, the Popes did not have a significant army and relied on Catholic countries to protect them militarily if required.

KEY EVENT

Peace of Campo Formio, 1798 The Treaty of Campo Formio ended Napoleon's Italian campaign. Its main significance was that the Austrians recognised the existence of the Cisalpine Republic.

Austrian control of Lombardy and its considerable influence over many of the other Italian states. As a result, in May 1796, the young French general **Napoleon Bonaparte** invaded northern Italy with the intention of sweeping out the Austrians. A series of French victories left Napoleon in control of most of northern Italy and from 1796 to 1799 he introduced a number of political changes.

- The regions of Lombardy, Modena, Bologna, Romagna and Ferrara were united into the Cisalpine Republic. This was administered on a model similar to that in France, with five directors and a legislature (Parliament). Unlike the French model however the legislature was appointed by Napoleon.
- The Republic of Genoa was transformed into the Republic of Liguria under French control.
- Until 1798, Piedmont was allowed to keep its monarchy, but lost Savoy and Nice to France. However, in 1799 Piedmont was annexed to France.
- In 1796, the French had invaded the **Papal States**, but it wasn't until 1798 that they intervened in Rome and deposed the Pope, Pius VI. A revolutionary Roman Republic was set up under French control. The Republic's constitution was modelled on that of the French.
- In 1797, Napoleon invaded Venice but handed it over to the Austrians as part of the **Peace of Campo Formio** of October 1798 in return for territory in Belgium.

French interest and Italian reaction

Some Italians, such as the *patrioti*, welcomed French rule. The *patrioti* supported the attacks on Church privileges and the destruction of old monarchies that took place after 1796. However, other Italians objected. In Naples in 1799, a revolt against French rule ended in the slaughter of thousands of middle-class supporters of the new order. In December 1798, a coalition of anti-French states was formed to push the French out of Italy. Known as the Second Coalition, it planned for Russian and Austrian armies to invade Italy. In April 1799, they invaded and defeated the French in a series of battles to the end of the year.

Despite this temporary setback for the French, it did not end their interest in Italy. Napoleon I had been away in

Egypt securing French control of parts of North Africa. On his return to France in late 1799, he seized political power by declaring himself First Consul and planned a new campaign in Italy. In May 1800, Napoleon led a large army across the Great St Bernard Pass and into northern Italy. He entered Milan, restored the Cisalpine Republic and moved rapidly to face a far larger Austrian army. At the Battle of Marengo on 14 June 1800, Napoleon won a great victory. This victory ensured French control of northern Italy for the next fourteen years. Again, the political map of the peninsula was redrawn.

- In 1805, the Cisalpine Republic became the Kingdom of Italy and Napoleon proclaimed himself its king. Napoleon chose as his viceroy his stepson, Eugene de Beauharnais.
- In 1805, the north-west regions of Italy (including Piedmont, Parma and Liguria) were incorporated into France and ruled as French *départements*. The importance of this was that these regions were exposed to the administrative reforms introduced in France, known as the **Code Napoleon**.
- The Central Duchies were amalgamated in 1801 into the Kingdom of Etruria, which was eventually annexed to France.
- Between 1805 and 1808, Napoleon's armies took over different parts of the Papal States. Then, in 1809, Napoleon declared that Rome was to be the 'Second City of the Empire' – that is, it would be incorporated into the French Empire. Pope Pius VII was to become a prisoner.

Napoleon was keen to give titles and land to as many of his relatives as he could. From 1806 the Kingdom of Naples was ruled by his brother Joseph, who became king. All feudal rights were abolished, a policy enforced by **Joachim Murat**. Sicily was not conquered by the French and was dominated by the British, who encouraged the introduction of a constitution in 1812 to be drawn up on British lines (in other words, there was a Parliament with two houses and a constitutional monarchy).

KEY TERM

Code Napoleon Under the code, feudalism (see Key term on page 23) was abolished and equality before the law established.

KEY PERSON

Joachim Murat (1767–1815) A flamboyant cavalry officer who succeeded Joseph as King of Naples in 1808. He married one of Napoleon's sisters, Caroline Bonaparte.

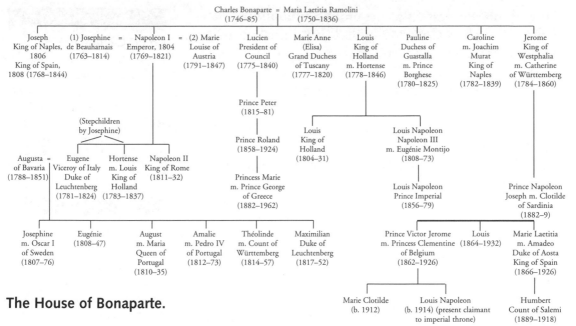

Charles Bonaparte = Maria Laetitia Ramolini
(1746–85)   (1750–1836)

Joseph
King of Naples,
1806
King of Spain,
1808 (1768–1844)

(1) Josephine = Napoleon I = (2) Marie
de Beauharnais   Emperor, 1804   Louise of
(1763–1814)   (1769–1821)   Austria
                                (1791–1847)

Lucien
President of
Council
(1775–1840)

Marie Anne
(Elisa)
Grand Duchess
of Tuscany
(1777–1820)

Louis
King of
Holland
m. Hortense
(1778–1846)

Pauline
Duchess of
Guastalla
m. Prince
Borghese
(1780–1825)

Caroline
m. Joachim
Murat
King of
Naples
(1782–1839)

Jerome
King of
Westphalia
m. Catherine
of Württemberg
(1784–1860)

Prince Peter
(1815–81)

Prince Roland
(1858–1924)

Princess Marie
m. Prince George
of Greece
(1882–1962)

(Stepchildren
by Josephine)

Augusta =
of Bavaria
(1788–1851)

Eugene
Viceroy of Italy
Duke of
Leuchtenberg
(1781–1824)

Hortense
m. Louis
King of
Holland
(1783–1837)

Napoleon II
King of Rome
(1811–32)

Louis
King of
Holland
(1804–31)

Louis Napoleon
Napoleon III
m. Eugénie Montijo
(1808–73)

Louis Napoleon
Prince Imperial
(1856–79)

Prince Napoleon
Joseph m. Clotilde
of Sardinia
(1882–9)

Josephine
m. Oscar I
of Sweden
(1807–76)

Eugénie
(1808–47)

August
m. Maria
Queen of
Portugal
(1810–35)

Amalie
m. Pedro IV
of Portugal
(1812–73)

Théolinde
m. Count of
Württemberg
(1814–57)

Maximilian
Duke of
Leuchtenberg
(1817–52)

Prince Victor Jerome
m. Princess Clementine
of Belgium
(1862–1926)

Louis
(1864–1932)

Marie Laetitia
m. Amadeo
Duke of Aosta
King of Spain
(1866–1926)

Marie Clotilde
(b. 1912)

Louis Napoleon
(b. 1914) (present claimant
to imperial throne)

Humbert
Count of Salemi
(1889–1918)

The House of Bonaparte.

IMPACT OF NAPOLEONIC RULE IN ITALY

Under French rule, many Italians experienced a transformation in how they were governed. Instead of a patchwork of customs and feudal laws that had dominated the running of so many of the states of Italy, they enjoyed the benefits of a new, more efficient, system. The French brought with them a fairer Code of Law. State officials administered parts of Italy under a unified and clearly defined system of rules. The Code forbade torture and stated that all people were equal in the eyes of the law. Even when the French were expelled from Italy and their laws repealed, it was difficult for many of the restored rulers to turn back the clock.

French rule sped up the process of the rise of the middle professional classes. In most regions of Italy before the 1790s, land was mainly owned by the aristocracy and the Church. However, Napoleonic rule meant the sale of large amounts of Church land. Those who benefited from this sale were not the peasants, but those who could afford to buy the land (which included the commercial and professional middle classes).

Many of the later leaders of the process of political unification such as **Count Camillo Cavour** came from families that made their fortunes in this period. Land sale also strengthened the position of members of the nobility, who were able to increase the size of their estates by buying Church land.

Popularity of French rule

The influence of the French revolution and the period of French dominance in Italy resulted in the emergence of secret societies. The societies were formed to plot against the French. When the French left Italy in 1814, they plotted against the restored governments. The stated aims of the **Carbonari** (the largest society) were the rejection of **absolutist government** and the protection of the rights of the people. After 1815, the secret societies were able to keep the idea of political reform alive even though change did not necessarily happen as a result of their activities.

However, French rule was by no means universally popular.

• The demands of war had meant that taxation was high.
• Many Italians were conscripted into the army of the Kingdom of Italy, which, by 1810, was some 50,000 strong.
• Many Italians fought all over Europe for Napoleon and for the ideas that revolutionary France stood for. These ideas – that there should be a strong, secular (non-religious) centralised state – would influence future generations of Italians.

Although demands for Italian unification were not strong in the opening years of the century, there had been a Kingdom of Italy, albeit one controlled from Paris.

The years of French dominance witnessed a serious attack on the Church as an institution. Although the Church was fully restored in 1815, the tradition of anti-clericalism (see pages 50–1) was one that lingered.

KEY PERSON

Count Camillo Cavour (1810–61) A Piedmontese statesman. He was prime minister from 1852–9, during which time he improved the economy. However, he resigned this position over the issue of Villafranca (see page 65).

KEY GROUP

The Carbonari The origins of this society are unclear, but translated the name means 'charcoal burners'. Every member of the society was sworn to secrecy in a special initiation ceremony. The Carbonari were committed to the principles of the rights of the people, and were prepared to use violence and revolution as the means by which it could achieve its aims. Although the Carbonari society was an international organisation, it was strongest in Naples where it had perhaps as many as 60,000 members.

KEY TERM

Absolutist government This occurs when a ruler rules without constraints, such as

Prince Klemens Metternich, a great influence in Italian affairs for a number of years.

a Parliament.

AFTERMATH OF THE NAPOLEONIC WARS

In 1815, the Napoleonic wars came to an end. The French Emperor Napoleon was banished to the island of St Helena in the Atlantic Ocean. Meanwhile, the victors of the war – Britain, Austria, Russia and Prussia – began to draw up a settlement that they hoped would ensure peace in Europe. Their task was not easy. French rule over much of Europe had seen boundaries redrawn and much political and social upheaval. The aim of the peacemakers was to return Europe to the days of political stability and to prevent France from ever causing such turmoil again.

One of the most influential peacemakers in 1815 was the Austrian foreign minister **Prince Klemens Metternich**. Indeed, he had considerable impact over Italian affairs for the next 30 years. In 1847, Prince Metternich commented that Italy was a mere 'geographical expression'. By this he meant that the idea of an Italian state was a fanciful one. For centuries the Italian peninsula was home to a number of distinct states with their own customs, governments, cultures and languages. In fact, the Italian language was only spoken by around 2.5 per cent of the population. The rest spoke in dialects.

The settlement of 1815, known as the Treaty of Vienna, reflected the diversity of Italy. Primarily, however, the Treaty reflected the wishes of Metternich and the desires of Austria, which now had even greater control over Italian affairs. This would be a most important development. Many of the demands for political change in Italy after 1815 were not necessarily from a desire to unite Italy but rather from a desire to destroy Austrian control and influence.

In 1815, Metternich's desire was to restore the old pre-1796 order and this fact was reflected in the terms of the Vienna Settlement. He wished to impose a conservative settlement thereby crushing the hopes of **liberals** and **nationalists** across Europe.

THE TREATY OF VIENNA AND ITS IMPACT

The Treaty had an impact on the following states.

The Kingdom of Sardinia (Piedmont). The Vienna treaty recognised the restoration of the House of Savoy as the rightful rulers of Piedmont. In 1814, **Victor Emmanuel I** returned to Piedmont and immediately began to restore the absolutist state. The Code Napoleon was repealed, as were various rights such as free and open trials. No laws passed after 1800 were recognised and the Church was restored to its pre-Napoleon privileged status. One important change introduced at Vienna was that the port and state of Genoa was granted to the House of Savoy.

Lombardy and Venice. Austrian dominance of Italian political life was assured by the return of Lombardy to Austrian control in 1814. However, it was strengthened by the recognition at Vienna of Austria's annexation of Venice.

The Papal States. By the terms of the Treaty of Vienna, Pope Pius VII was restored to his position as spiritual and temporal ruler of the Papal States. The Code Napoleon was abolished in most parts of the Papal States and the papal legal codes re-established. However, such a move was not universal. In Emilia-Romagna the Code Napoleon remained. Austrian influence over the region was considerably increased by the fact that Austrian armed forces were to be stationed in the Papal States. These forces were a sign that Austria would, if necessary, use force to protect the conservative settlement imposed on Italy.

The Central Duchies. The Treaty of Vienna left the Central Duchies firmly under Austrian influence. Grand Duke Ferdinand III, brother of the Austrian Emperor, became ruler of Tuscany. However, this did not mean that he was as conservative or as repressive as some of the other Restoration rulers. Indeed, Ferdinand and his first minister, Victor Fossombroni, improved education, set up hospitals and food relief during the outbreak of typhus in 1815–16, and allowed **freedom of expression**, which was not allowed in the rest of Italy.

KEY GROUP

The Jesuits Founded in the sixteenth century in response to the Protestant reformation, the Society of Jesus (otherwise known as the Jesuits) became the shock troops of the Catholic Church. This meant that they would act to promote Catholicism wherever it was under threat. The Jesuits were the arch-enemies of those who opposed the power and influence of the Catholic Church.

KEY PEOPLE

Marie Louise (1791–1847)
Daughter of the Austrian emperor Francis I. She became Napoleon's wife in 1810 and was to remain so until his death in 1821.

Ferdinand I (1751–1825)
Ferdinand I was made King of Naples in 1759 at the age of nine when his father, Charles IV, became King of Spain. He was forced to flee his kingdom in 1798 when it was conquered by the French. Ferdinand married Maria Carolina the daughter of the Austrian Empress Marie Teresa. Maria dominated the marriage and the direction of government policy.

The new ruler of Parma, **Marie Louise** of Bourbon-Parma, was equally broadminded. She scrapped the Code Napoleon in 1820, but replaced it with something similar. This was no surprise given the fact that she had been Napoleon's wife! In Modena, Duke Francis IV was far more repressive, reinstating the **Jesuit** order's influence over the lives of the Modenese.

The Kingdom of Naples. The Bourbon King, **Ferdinand I**, was restored to his throne in 1815 with vague promises of maintaining some of the legacy of French and British influence in Naples and Sicily respectively. However, this was not to be the case. The Church was restored to its position of power and authority. Many of the liberal projects introduced by the French such as road building and extending education were abandoned. In Sicily in 1816, the British-inspired constitution was destroyed – much to the frustration of many of the nobility, who had enjoyed the power it had given them.

CONCLUSION

- The Vienna Settlement failed to wipe out all traces of Napoleonic rule in Italy.
- However, Austrian influence over Italy was considerable and Metternich's insistence that all traces of liberal government be suppressed was generally followed.
- There was little, if no, agitation for a form of united Italy. However, there were a number of Italians who hoped for an end to absolutist monarchy.
- The secret societies in particular were prepared to act in the name of change.

SUMMARY QUESTIONS

1 What were the most important consequences of Napoleonic rule for the cause of Italian nationalism?

2 What did the Vienna Settlement aim to achieve in Italy?

CHAPTER 2

What happened in the revolutions of the 1820s and 1830s?

INTRODUCTION

Although in the 1820s there were no national movements pressing for Italian unity, there were groups with serious grievances against the type of rule re-introduced after 1815. Some of the discontented joined the secret societies. Those who had lost out from the restoration of old monarchies, including purged army officers and civil servants, were more keen on radical action. Some wished for the restoration of lost political rights and constitutions that would guarantee those rights.

A number of uprisings and revolutions in the 1820s and 1830s reflect a dissatisfaction with several rulers. But this dissatisfaction often had causes related to local issues. The revolutions that took place were to challenge the legitimacy and rule of some of the restored rulers. However, they did not go so far as to challenge Austrian **hegemony**. Neither did they form the basis of a movement demanding change on a national basis.

KEY TERM

Hegemony From the Greek, meaning 'to lead'. It is the acceptance of the values and norms of the ruling classes by a large section of society.

THE REVOLUTIONS OF 1820–1

Naples

The restoration of the Bourbon monarchy in Naples was not without considerable problems. Ferdinand I and his chief minister Luigi de Medici introduced several measures that resulted in the most serious challenge to the restoration settlement to date. In 1818, Ferdinand restored the Church to a position of power and influence in Naples. Many Neapolitans were offended by the fact that the Church was given powers of censorship.

The Bourbon monarchy was in financial difficulty after 1815.

- It had to pay for the Austrian army of occupation and reparations were imposed by Austria.
- By the Treaty of Vienna, Ferdinand was even obliged to pay compensation to the French viceroy, Eugene de Beauharnais, for loss of office.

The result of a heavy financial burden was cutbacks in government spending.

During the British occupation of Sicily, the port of Palermo had flourished. However, a fall in agricultural prices had hit the port, as had the fall in trade. Union with Naples in 1815 was unpopular with many who disliked the absolutist Bourbons. The repeal of the Sicilian–British style constitution in 1816 was a source of considerable grievance for many.

In both Naples and Sicily, liberals had hoped that the return of the Bourbons might bring with it a constitution that would guarantee political liberties. The trigger for revolution was the news from Spain of an uprising that had resulted in the promise of just such a constitution.

The Spanish revolt, 1820

In 1814, the Spanish King Ferdinand VII had been restored to the throne promising that he would respect the liberal constitution of 1812. It soon became clear that this was not the case. Instead, Ferdinand persecuted liberals and ruled in such a way that many within the army became unhappy. In 1820, a revolt broke out led by Colonel Rafael Rigo. The movement gathered pace until Ferdinand yielded and restored the constitution.

The Neapolitan revolt, 1820

In July 1820, an attempted revolution took place in Naples. However, the scale of the revolution was small: led by 30 members of the Carbonari supported by 100 soldiers from the local garrison. As the revolutionaries set out for the town of Avellino, their ranks were swelled by more members of the Carbonari rather than by peasants.

The success of the uprising relied on the actions of an army officer, General Guglielmo Pepe, who led three regiments of soldiers in support of their cause (rather than against the revolutionaries). The result was that, on 6 July, King Ferdinand agreed to a new constitution. The next day, he clarified that this would be based on the **Spanish Constitution model of 1812**.

So it seemed that the revolutionaries had succeeded. Pepe was put in charge of the army and a new government was sworn in that included a number of ministers from the Carbonari. However, the new government was quickly undermined by its own weaknesses. The Carbonari briefly won support as the rumours spread that it was on the verge of seizing Church property. But this was not the case. The Carbonari were divided among themselves and had no policies beyond the demand for a constitution.

Revolution in Sicily, 1821

Stories of the uprising in Naples spread to Sicily. There was considerable unrest in the capital Palermo. The cry went up in support of the introduction of a new constitution. The revolution was led by the workers of Palermo who belonged to the guilds of the city (known as the *maestranze*). There was little in their demands that suggested any nationalist sentiment. Indeed, the revolution was confined to Palermo and others in Sicily showed little sympathy for the cause of their revolutionary neighbours. Across the Straits of Messina, the new Neapolitan government also felt it necessary to restrain their revolutionary comrades, even if that meant using military force.

The events in the south of Italy did not go unnoticed in the rest of Europe. The revolutionary uprisings worried the Austrian foreign minister Prince Metternich to the extent that he called an international congress at Troppau in October 1820 to discuss the issue. Metternich was the sworn enemy of revolutionary activity across Europe. The **Troppau Doctrine**, although agreed by the eastern powers, was not accepted by Britain.

In January 1821, Metternich called another Congress, this time at Laibach. He invited Ferdinand to attend, which he

KEY TERMS

The Spanish Constitution, 1812 This introduced a democratic structure to Spain that was advanced for its time. The main features of the constitution included a one-house Parliament elected by universal suffrage.

Maestranze A division of 72 guilds (organisations based on trades), each fiercely protective of its own privileges. The *maestranze* had little sympathy for the middle classes or liberals. One of its first revolutionary actions was to murder members of the 1812 government.

The Troppau Doctrine, 1820 Prussia, Austria and Russia agreed that it was the duty of the Great Powers to intervene militarily to support any government overthrown by revolution.

duly did. Once out of Naples, Ferdinand renounced the constitution and asked the Austrians for military support to crush his own government. In March 1821, Austrian troops entered Naples and the revolutionary government was crushed. Ferdinand unleashed a wave of **repression**, which saw a number of the Carbonari publicly executed. The importance of the Austrians as the ultimate arbitrators of Italian political life could clearly be seen.

Revolt in Piedmont, 1821

The diverse and localist nature of the secret societies such as the Carbonari can be seen by what happened next in Piedmont. In Naples, the Carbonari pushed for a constitution. In Piedmont, their demands were different in some ways. The restoration under Victor Emmanuel I had seen a return to autocratic and conservative monarchy. The Carbonari in Piedmont was made up of professional men and military officers who believed that the introduction of a **constitutional monarchy** would make possible their ultimate aim – the destruction of Austrian influence in Italy. The means by which such a change could take place was revolution. The revolutionaries pinned their hopes for a constitutional monarchy on the second in line to the throne, **Charles Albert**, Prince of Carignan.

The Neapolitan uprising of 1820 was an inspiration to a group of Piedmontese army officers who, in March 1821, seized the fortress of Alessandria and declared a provisional government. The revolution spread. In Turin, the army mutinied and Victor Emmanuel abdicated in favour of his brother, Charles Felix. The problem was that Charles Felix had left Piedmont on a visit to Modena. Therefore the next in line, Charles Albert, was appointed **regent**.

It is important to stop the story at this point to look more closely at the actions of the Piedmontese rebels. Some of their actions seem to point to the existence of a national sentiment, a desire for an Italian nation state.

- The revolutionaries declared that the king (Charles Albert) should be declared 'King of Italy'.
- Their demands were made 'in the name of the **Italian Federation**'.

- They were nationally minded in the fact that they wanted to expel the Austrians from Italy.

However, one should not exaggerate the extent of a national movement. The stress laid by the revolutionaries on the idea of Italy was mainly in response to the presence of Austria on Italian soil.

As regent, Charles Albert issued a constitution as demanded by the revolutionaries. However, on his return from Modena, Charles Felix was quick to reject any idea of a constitution. Indeed, he stated that he would not accept any change in 'the form of government' and promptly asked Metternich for military support. Charles Albert fled, recognising that the cause of political reform was a lost one. A number of revolutionaries under the command of Santorre di Satarosa raised an army, but it was defeated at Novara in April 1821 by a combination of Austrian and Piedmontese troops. Again, it was clear that Austria's domination was the most important factor in deciding the political fate of Italians. It was also clear that Piedmont was to be ruled in an autocratic manner by Charles Felix until his death in 1831.

THE REVOLUTIONS OF 1831

A number of Italian revolutionaries fled abroad after the failure of the 1820–1 uprisings. Many ended up in Paris and some even took part in the July Days uprising in France in 1830. The French king, Charles X, was overthrown by a mixture of radicals, liberals and the Paris mob. He was replaced by Louis Philippe, who promised to act as a constitutional monarch. To liberals in Italy, the revolution in France raised the possibility of French support for a similar revolution in Italy. Such support, in their view, would act as a counter-balance to the power of conservative Austria.

Modena
The uprising in Modena was led by **Enrico Misley**. Misley's motivation for provoking revolution was primarily the achievement of Italian freedom from Austrian domination. He tried to enlist the support of the Duke of

Modena, Francesco IV, by promising him support in becoming King of Italy. Initially, Francesco seemed interested. But he was acutely aware of the danger of challenging Austrian power.

Two days before the revolution was due to begin in February 1831, Francesco had Ciro Menotti, one of the important members of the conspiracy, arrested. However, revolution did go ahead in Bologna and quickly spread to Modena. Francesco fled to Vienna to plead for support from Metternich. While he was there, he heard news that the ruler of neighbouring Parma, Marie Louise, had fled in the face of similar demands for a constitution. However, revolutionary excitement did not last long. In March 1831, Francesco returned to the Central Duchies with an Austrian army and the revolutionaries were crushed. Many such as Menotti were executed.

Revolution in the Papal States

Much more threatening to the established order in Italy was the outbreak of revolution in 1831 in the Papal States. Although not touched by the 1821 revolutions, there was repression of liberals and the secret societies were weaker than they were further south in Naples.

- In 1825, Leo XII was elected Pope. He immediately imposed a strict clerical regime.
- In 1829, Leo XII died. He was succeeded by Pius VIII.
- In 1830, Pius died after less than a year in office.

Challenge to the clerical state. As revolution raged in the Grand Duchies, so its leader Menotti urged an uprising in the Papal States. A brief attempt at revolution by Louis Napoleon Bonaparte (Napoleon III) in Rome was a failure. However, a more serious reaction to clerical rule emerged. The aim of those who rose was not to create a united Italy, but to challenge the clerical state and to re-establish a secular state similar to that under Napoleonic rule.

The revolutionaries. The aims of the revolutionaries in the Papal States in 1831 tells us much about the weakness of Italian nationalism in the period. Unlike Menotti, who had a vision of a revolution leading to the creation of some form of nation state, the revolutionaries in the Papal States wished for liberal reforms. It is accurate to describe their actions as those of revolutionaries. However, it is best to call this 'revolutionary liberalism' rather than 'nationalism'. The leaders of this moderate revolution were from the middle and artisan classes.

A new constitution. In February 1831, a revolutionary army led by Colonel Giuseppe Sercognani captured the papal port of Ancona and the Umbrian capital Perugia. In March 1831, a provisional government led by the elderly Giovanni Vicini was set up in Bologna. In March 1831, it issued a constitution promising the following.

- A reformed finance system with moderated tariffs.
- An elected assembly that would chose a president and cabinet.
- A fairer judicial system based on the Napoleonic model.

This was not particularly radical, but it was too much for the Austrians. For Metternich, revolutionary liberalism was as much a threat to the established order as revolutionary nationalism.

Further revolutions. In March 1831, an Austrian army intervened and took Bologna with relative ease. The revolutionary army surrendered to papal forces believing the papal intermediary Cardinal Benvenuti when he promised an amnesty for all those who had taken up arms against papal rule. They were mistaken to trust Benvenuti. Papal armies swept through the **Marches** acting in a manner that was to sow the seeds for further revolution.

During the Second Empire the French economy flourished. However, **Louis Napoleon Bonaparte** was to be undone by the diplomacy of the Prussian Chancellor Bismarck, who lured him into war in 1870. Defeat at Sedan sealed his political fate and he was deposed by the Paris mob. He died in exile in England in 1871.

Conclusion

With hindsight one should judge that the revolutions of 1831 were a hopeless cause. They failed for a number of reasons.

KEY AREA

The Marches is the region in the east of central Italy. It stretches from the Apennine Mountains to the Adriatic Sea.

KEY PERSON

Louis Napoleon Bonaparte, Napoleon III (1808–73)
The nephew of Napoleon Bonaparte (Napoleon I). As a young adult he attempted to incite revolution in Italy and France, and in 1840 he was sentenced to life in prison. He escaped from prison in 1846 and made his way to England. However, he returned to France in order to take part in the February Revolution of 1848. In the same year he was elected President of the Second Republic. Louis Napoleon's power was consolidated by the elevation of his status to Emperor in 1852.

- They did not constitute a national uprising, but were regionally based revolts.
- There was little if no communication of support from revolutionaries in one region such as Bologna for those in another such as Modena. This was partly because the ambitions of the revolutionaries were limited by their localism.
- The social base of the revolutionaries was narrow. As already noted above, Misely was an academic, Menotti a prosperous businessman. The revolutionaries of 1831 did not have a broad popular support. Often they were members of exclusive secret societies such as the Carbonari. Because of their social background, the revolutionaries were not attempting a social revolution. In most cases their aims were constitutional, to extend power to their class through the granting of a constitution.
- Most importantly, the revolutionaries of 1831 failed to attract foreign support to counteract the impact of Austria. Misley had hoped for support from the government of the French king **Louis Philippe**, who had only recently been brought to power by a similar type of liberal revolution. However, Louis Philippe quickly dashed the hopes of the revolutionaries by stating clearly that it was not the responsibility of the French to interfere in other countries' affairs. The problem was that this **policy of non-intervention** was also adopted by those in one part of Italy who identified themselves through their region and argued that it was not in their interests to fight for the cause of other Italians in other parts of the country. Without the support of a foreign power the revolutionaries had little chance of standing up to the might of the Austrians.

KEY PERSON

Louis Philippe (1773–1850) Born in Paris, he became known as the 'Citizen King'. He reigned from 1830 to 1848. In 1848, when the Paris mob rose he abdicated and fled to England.

KEY THEME

Policy of non-intervention In 1831, Louis Philippe's minister Casimir Perrier stated: 'We do not recognise the right of any people to force us to fight in its cause; the blood of Frenchmen belongs to France alone.'

SUMMARY QUESTIONS

1 Why did the revolutions of 1820 and 1831 fail?

2 What was the significance of the secret societies?

3 What was the importance of Austria in Italy in this period?

CHAPTER 3

Why was the *Risorgimento* important?

INTRODUCTION

The roots of an Italian national identity go back to the Roman Empire. During the Middle Ages, when Italy was divided politically into a number of small states, there were still those who thought in terms of Italy as a cultural identity at least. Most important of these was the writer **Dante**, who wrote in terms of *Italia* as a country. In the sixteenth century, one of the foremost Italian philosophers, **Niccolò Machiavelli**, wrote of *Italia* as a cultural entity. Neither wrote in terms of Italy as a nation state, because such an idea did not exist during their lifetimes. It was only in the late eighteenth and nineteenth centuries that awareness of national identity began to have political significance.

EIGHTEENTH- AND NINETEENTH-CENTURY WRITERS ON THE *RISORGIMENTO*

The term '*Risorgimento*' was first used in the context of national identity by S. Bettinelli in his cultural history of Italy entitled *Del Risorgimento d'Italia dopo il mille* (1775). In the same period, the writer Vittorio Alfieri wrote in terms of national identity. The historian Carlo Denina wrote in his book *The Revolutions of Italy* (1770) about Italy as a whole rather than just Venice or Piedmont. One should not exaggerate the impact of these writers. Their audience was small, mainly consisting of members of the upper class. However, their works contained some common themes.

- They wrote about the *Risorgimento* in terms of a moral revival – the struggle of good over evil.
- They also linked the resurrection of the culture of the Italian people with the concept of liberty.

The writer Dante, who had an important cultural influence on Italy.

THE FIRST REVOLUTIONS OF THE *RISORGIMENTO*

The ideas of liberty were strengthened by events in France in the late-1780s and 1790s. This marks the beginning of a new phase of the *Risorgimento*, moving from a cultural-literary era to one in which political solutions were proposed.

In France, **Jacobins** spoke in terms of justice, liberty and the brotherhood of man. Italian Jacobins were involved in plots to overthrow the government in Naples and Turin in 1794. Mainly educated people, they spoke in terms of liberty for the Italian people that could only be achieved with the destruction of autocracy. These were the first revolutions of the *Risorgimento* and the leading participants paid heavily with their lives.

- In 1794, three leaders of the uprising in Naples (including 21 year-old Emanuele de Deo) were shot.
- In 1795, another Jacobin-inspired revolt led to the hanging of its leader Francesco Di Blasi.

THE DESIRE FOR CHANGE

Not all Italians who wanted political change were revolutionaries. Several were moderate in their tactics and their aims. Indeed, the ambitions of many such as Francesco Melzi d'Eril, who briefly led the government in Milan, was limited to the demand for a greater share in ruling their regions. They were not concerned with revolutionary upheaval or with the creation of an Italian state. Instead they hoped for:

- a more efficient administration
- the removal of the last elements of **feudalism**
- the introduction of limited social reform such as primary education.

The importance of these individuals was in their desire for change, despite the fact that it was limited in its ambition.

'La Liberta insidiata dalla Tirannide' (Liberty resists the Tyranny).

THE SECRET SOCIETIES

The period of French dominance in Italy (see pages 6–10) was to lead to the development of secret societies, whose members became disillusioned with, then actively opposed, French rule.

The Carbonari

The liberty that many Italians had hoped for did not materialise. The significance of groups such as the Carbonari was that they believed liberty could only be achieved with political change, either with the removal of the French or, after 1814, through revolution against the restored monarchies. Although the Carbonari were the largest secret society, there were others whose role in maintaining the revolutionary tradition should not be ignored.

The Adelfi

The Adelfi was a strongly anti-French society, which transformed itself into the strangely named 'Sublime Perfect Masters' in 1818. Its main aim was the destruction of Austrian rule that would lead to a democratic republic. The leader of the Sublime Perfect Masters was **Filippo Buonarrotti**, who was an experienced revolutionary. The society's membership was based in the north, which

KEY PERSON

Filippo Buonarrotti (1761–1837) The problem for historians in weighing up the significance of certain individuals in developing the ideas of national unity is that the secret societies were, not surprisingly, very secretive. Buonarrotti was considered an important enemy of Austria by Metternich, who commented that he directed 'the greater part of the secret societies of Europe' for many years. But one should not exaggerate his importance. The organisation that he led, the Sublime Perfect Masters, was based in Geneva, not Italy.

Giuseppe Mazzini, the founder of Young Italy.

explains why the expulsion of Austria from Italian soil was considered the primary objective.

The Italian Federation

The secret society named the 'Italian Federation' was led by Count Confalonieri. It aimed for the creation of a north Italian state to be ruled by a constitutional monarchy.

YOUNG ITALY

It was the failure of the secret societies in the 1820s and 1830s revolutions that led to the founding of a new organisation, **Young Italy**, by **Giuseppe Mazzini**. This new organisation did not reject all aspects of the secret societies. It looked after its members, and gave them passwords, uniforms and ritual. However, there were differences in both organisation and philosophy that were to make Young Italy distinct.

- The organisation was accompanied by a journal edited by Mazzini, also entitled *Young Italy*. This journal was important in spreading Mazzinian ideas.
- At the heart of Mazzini's ideas was a belief in democracy and that the will of the people – *la plebe* – should be listened to. In his view, God's Will was expressed through the people and therefore their demands mirrored the demands of the Lord.
- In Mazzini's view, the will of the people was to live in an independent nation of 'free men and equals'. To achieve this independent nation it was necessary to engage in a national revolution.
- Where Mazzini differed was in the breadth of his vision. He did not just see a union of northern Italian states, as did so many other patriots. He envisaged a union of all Italian-speaking provinces – including the south, Sicily and Sardinia. In 1829, he clearly summarised his vision: 'The fatherland of an Italian is not Rome, Florence or Milan but the whole of Italy.'
- Young Italy was republican in its views. This did not mean that Mazzini dismissed out of hand constitutional monarchies. These were, in his view, useful as a stepping

stone – 'governments of transition' – on the way to the ideal: a united Italian republic. Indeed, in 1831 Mazzini wrote to the King of Piedmont, Charles Albert, asking him to put himself at the head of the movement for a united Italy. In his letter, Mazzini asked that the king lead the nation and put on his banner 'Union, Liberty, Independence'.

The failures of Young Italy

The ideas of Young Italy were spread from Marseilles in France (Mazzini's base) to Piedmont, the Papal States and Tuscany. In Piedmont, the readership of *Young Italy* grew and new adherents to the cause of revolution were recruited. However, the attempts at revolution ended in farce.

- In 1833, a proposed army *coup* was detected before it could begin. The response of Charles Albert's government was ferocious. Twelve members of Young Italy were executed out of 67 people arrested.
- In 1834, a planned attack on Piedmont fizzled out before it started. An uprising in Genoa scheduled for February 1834 and led by a new recruit to the Young Italy movement, **Guiseppe Garibaldi**, also failed to get off the ground.

Such failures made Young Italy a laughing stock throughout Italy. Mazzini lived in Switzerland from 1834 to 1837, then moved to London where he lived for the next twelve years. His importance and influence are examined more closely in Section 1 (see pages 100–106). However, it is important to point out that although his attempts at revolution in the 1830s seemed to be feeble and unrealistic, his ideas, even at this stage, were an inspiration to others. One such example can be seen in the actions of **Attilio and Emilio Bandera**.

REGIONAL DISTINCTIONS AND MEANS OF EXPRESSION

The revolutions of the 1820s and 1830s were regionally (rather than nationally) based. As we have seen on pages

KEY PEOPLE

Guiseppe Garibaldi (1807–82) Garibaldi was the most famous soldier and patriot of the *Risorgimento*. Born in Nice he became a follower of Mazzini and had to flee Italy in the 1830s. He went to South America where he became involved in a number of wars. He returned to Italy in 1848 and, although a republican, joined with Charles Albert of Piedmont in his attempt to free Italy of Austrian rule. He led the army of the ill-fated Roman Republic in 1849 and after its collapse he fled to the United States of America. In 1860, he played an important part in the unification of Italy by conquering the Kingdom of the Two Sicilies with his army of soldiers known as the Red Shirts. He was involved in two attempts to take Rome by force in the 1860s and in 1874 was elected to the Italian Parliament. He was the hero of his day.

Attilio and Emilio Bandera Officers in the Austrian Navy. They eventually deserted and launched an invasion of Calabria in 1844. The problem was that there were only nineteen of them and their numbers had swelled by two by the time the authorities arrived. The Bandera brothers were shot, but in their death they became important martyrs for the cause of national unity.

14–21, most were tragic – almost farcical – failures rather than serious attempts at seizing power. But patriots in different parts of Italy continued to express themselves to their neighbours in distinct ways.

- In Tuscany, the ideas of national identity were spread in the pages of the journal *Antologia* (see Key Term on page 12).
- In the years following the restoration of Austrian control of Lombardy, there were those who encouraged the use of Italian as part of their expression of the importance of national identity.
- The Italian language periodical *Biblioteca Italiana* was founded in Milan in 1816. Indeed, such journals were crucial to the spread of the idea of an Italian identity and national consciousness.
- Equally important as the *Biblioteca* was the journal *Il Politecnico*, which was produced in Milan between 1839 and 1845.

The Austrian rulers of Lombardy were prepared to tolerate the publication of such journals because they were not openly political. But that was not the point. Such journals raised consciousness of a common culture among the educated classes.

THE CREATION OF NATIONAL ORGANISATIONS

Equally important in the development of an Italian national consciousness was the creation of national rather than regional organisations, such as the *Congresso degli Scienziata* (Congress of Science). The *Congresso* held meetings in different parts of Italy between 1839 and 1847. Crucially, these meetings were attended by delegates from many different regions. The topics discussed were wide ranging, from the latest medical research to agricultural innovation. Importantly, the language used at the meetings was Italian and there was a political edge to their agenda. At a *Congresso* meeting held in Genoa in 1846, the occasion was used to celebrate the victory of Italian arms over the Austrians in 1746.

Many of the future heroes of the *Risorgimento* attended the *Congresso*. They provided a function as a nursery for more moderate (in comparison to Mazzinian) nationalist opinion.

PATRIOTIC THEMES IN MUSIC AND LITERARY WORKS

In the 1840s, the *Risorgimento* was marked by the increase of cultural works with patriotic themes.

Music
The most famous Italian operatic composer was **Giuseppe Verdi**. In the work he composed in the 1840s there were clear political messages.

- The opera *Nabucco* (first performed in 1842 in Milan) included the famous stirring 'Chorus of the Hebrew Slaves'. The parallel to be drawn between the enslavement of the Israelites and the repression of the Italians was clear for many in the audience.
- Equally nationalistic was the opera *I Lombardi*, first performed in 1843.

The performance of Verdi's works became synonymous with anti-Austrian sentiment. Such was the impact of Verdi on nationalist opinion that, at times of tension, performances of his work caused outbursts of violence between Italian patriots and Austrian army officers.

Literary works
Throughout the 1840s, a number of literary works helped to define even further the Italian national identity and provoke debate among nationally minded Italians about the future of the country.

The Mazzinians still hoped for a unitary state brought about by revolution, but many more 'moderate' Italians believed that the way forward was for a federation of Italian states. The roots of these federal ideas was the fact that economic growth in Lombardy and other areas had meant that significant numbers of middle-class Italians saw closer economic ties between the Italian regions as progress.

Primato Morale e Civile degli Italiani. In 1843, the publication of *Primato Morale e Civile degli Italiani* ('On the Moral and Civil Primacy of the Italians') by **Vincenzo Gioberti** was to have an important impact on opinion in Italy. Gioberti agreed with Mazzini that Italy should be rid of foreign influence, both French and Austrian. However, he thought Mazzini was mad and his tactics damaging. Instead, in *Primato* Gioberti outlined a more moderate approach to ensuring Italian liberty.

- He argued that the Italian states should be drawn together in a federation under the leadership of the Pope. He believed that it was the papacy in Rome that gave Italians the moral upper hand over other European peoples.
- This line of thought became known as **neo-Guelph**. It appealed to many as it offered a way forward without revolution. It particularly appealed to those who disliked the idea of a French-style unitary state as suggested by Mazzini and his followers.
- The weakness of Gioberti's book was that it failed to mention the issue of Austrian control of Lombardy or Venetia and the fact that papal rule of the Papal States had not exactly been popular or effective.

Gioberti's views appealed to Italian Catholics but were not universally popular. A group of Italian writers, including Guiseppe La Farina, wrote attacking papal power. However, the most important legacy of the *Primato* was to introduce the idea of a papal-led resolution to the national question. This was to have an important effect on a priest named Giovanni Maria Mastai-Feretti who, in 1846, was elected as Pope Pius IX.

Le Speranze d'Italia. The publication of *Primato* was to serve as an inspiration to others. In 1844, **Cesare Balbo**'s *Le Speranze d'Italia* ('The Hopes of Italy') was published. Balbo was a great admirer of the works of Gioberti and dedicated his book to him. In *Le Speranze d'Italia*, Balbo predicted many of the diplomatic and political developments of the coming years.

- Like Gioberti, Balbo argued in favour of a federation of states. However, his view of Italy was limited to the north. While accepting the importance of the papacy, Balbo suggested that the Piedmontese monarchy should take the lead in expelling the Austrians from Lombardy and Venice.

- Most significantly, Balbo argued that the solutions to the dilemmas facing Italian nationalists would not be found in revolution but through Italian and European diplomacy.
- Balbo felt that if **Austria** were to be pushed out of Italy, it could look east to **the Balkans** for territory and influence. This was to be a prophetic suggestion.

As with Gioberti, Balbo failed to address the issue of what would happen when the Austrians decided they did not want to move out of Lombardy. However, his book became very popular in Piedmont and especially at the court of the Piedmontese king, Charles Albert.

Degli Ultimi Casi di Romagna. Another important influence in strengthening the more conservative argument for political change was Massimo d'Azeglio. In September 1845, D'Azeglio was to witness first hand an attempted revolution in Romagna in the Papal States. The following year he published his account of the revolution in *Degli Ultimi Casi di Romagna* ('On Recent Events in Romagna'). D'Azeglio was very clear in his conclusions.

- Those who had died in the Romagna revolution should be treated as martyrs, because they had fought against Austrian and Papal tyranny. However, he argued that revolution was not the way forward.
- Balbo and **D'Azeglio** agreed that **public opinion** and European opinion were crucial. If it was well informed and positive, then change would come about naturally.

CONCLUSION

By the mid-1840s, the ideas of national identity had began to move towards ideas of national unity. There were common themes among Italian patriots, most obviously the desire to destroy Austrian influence and interference in

KEY AREA

Austria and the Balkans
In 1866, Austria handed Venice over to the new Italian state after its defeat by the Prussians in the Austro-Prussian war. Although it was to hold on to Italian land (known as the irredentist lands) in the north such as Trent and Trieste, Austria did turn its attention to the Balkans for influence – for example, in 1908 it annexed Bosnia Herzogovina.

KEY THEME

D'Azeglio and public opinion In one of his most famous phrases, D'Azeglio argued for 'a conspiracy of public opinion in broad daylight'. However, this could not be done overnight. In another much used quote, D'Azeglio argued that 'to make Italy out of Italians, one must not be in a hurry'.

Italy. However, there were different strands of thought about how this might take place. Most important were:

- Mazzinian ideas of revolution leading to a unitary Italian state, preferably a republic
- moderate opinion in favour of a more gradual approach resulting in constitutional government
- neo-Guelph ideas of a federal state under the direction of the papacy.

The events of 1848–9 were to decide the most likely means by which change would take place.

SUMMARY QUESTIONS

1 What are the main themes of the *Risorgimento*?

2 How did Mazzini, Gioberti and D'Azeglio differ in their proposals for change in Italy?

CHAPTER 4

What happened in the revolutions of 1848–9?

INTRODUCTION

There were many causes of the revolutions that spread across Italy and beyond during 1848–9. The hopes and expectations of liberals for reform were heightened by the election of **Pius IX** in 1846. Added to this was the clamour of nationalists for the destruction of Austrian power, which increased as the Austrian Empire seemingly faltered. Agitation was increased by the economic crisis that swept Europe in 1846–7 as a result of harvest failure in 1846. For eighteen months the Italian peninsula was in turmoil until the gains won by liberals were reversed and the revolutions that had taken place were suppressed.

KEY PERSON

Pius IX (1792–1878)
Pope from 1846 to 1878, Pius IX was one of the most influential figures of the *Risorgimento*. His parents wanted him to have a career in the military, but his health was not deemed sufficiently robust. Instead he became a priest and a cardinal in 1839.

CAUSES OF THE REVOLUTIONS, 1848

The reforms of Pope Pius IX
In 1846, Pope Gregory XVI died. He was succeeded by Cardinal Mastai Ferretti, who chose the title Pius IX.

Pope Pius IX, elected in 1846. He became a leading figure of the *Risorgimento*.

Immediately, Pius extended a hand of reconciliation to the liberals by declaring an amnesty for political offences, releasing some 2000 prisoners from papal gaols. Such a move impressed the liberals, as did Pius' appointment of the liberal Cardinal Gizzi as his Secretary of State. A number of reforms followed.

- In 1847, press censorship by the Church was ended and censorship in the Papal States was undertaken by a committee of predominantly laymen. This move allowed the creation of a freer press in the Papal States that was to have important consequences later on.
- A civic guard of local people was created to protect property. The guard was armed. The guard quickly gained members who were sympathisers of Mazzinian demands for a republic.
- A Council of State, the *Consulta*, was set up in 1847 to advise the papacy on how to run the Papal States. Although its powers were limited, to many liberals it was the first step on the road to the elected Parliament they so desired.

The motivation of Pius IX in allowing these reforms was to make papal rule more effective and popular (although the former criteria was by far and away the most important). However, in doing so he appeared to be a 'liberal pope', something that Metternich in particular found very worrying.

Metternich's reaction to the Pope's reforms

The reaction of Metternich to the reforms of Pius IX was predictable and important. Under the Treaty of Vienna the Austrians were given the right to keep an army in the town of Ferrara, despite the fact that it was inside the Papal States. In July 1847, the city was occupied by Austrian troops. Pius IX responded in a way that raised his reputation with Italian nationalists to even greater heights.

- He lodged a formal protest with the Austrian government claiming that the sovereignty of the Papal States had been infringed.
- He proposed a customs union of Italian states in which trade could take place without tariffs (taxes) being

imposed. A treaty was signed in November 1847 with Tuscany and Piedmont, but which left out the states controlled by Austria.

The impact of Pius IX's reforms in other parts of Italy was considerable. In Piedmont and Tuscany, for example, there was unrest and demands for change. The response of Charles Albert in Piedmont in October 1847 was to sack his conservative minister, Solara della Margarita, and announce a package of limited reforms. However, the emphasis should be on the word 'limited', because Charles Albert was not suddenly preparing to introduce a liberal government. None the less, he did allow press censorship to be relaxed and local government was reorganised.

As is often the case, granting reform did little to satisfy liberals and radicals who simply increased their **demands for reform**. The same applied to Tuscany where Duke Leopold II introduced limited reforms that served to encourage radicals to demand a constitution.

Economic problems

Agitation for political reform was partly the result of economic problems in Italy during 1846–7. In particular, the poor harvest led to food riots from north to south and made deep-rooted economic problems worse.

- In southern areas such as Calabria, land enclosure had taken **common land** from the peasantry. Their response was violence.
- In the north, under-employment in the textile industries resulted in workers destroying machinery.

So the initial cause of unrest was social. But the unrest soon turned into a political demonstration, stirred by a free press.

Uprising in Sicily

The uprising in Sicily in 1848 was not caused by any demands for national unity. Instead, it was a reaction against the repressive regime of Ferdinand II. In 1836, an outbreak of **cholera** on the island killed one-tenth of the Sicilian population (some 65,000 people) and led to the

Demands for reform
Liberals in the north of Italy were encouraged by events in Switzerland in 1847, during which forces in favour of the introduction of a liberal constitution defeated the more conservative alliance known as the *Sonderbund*.

KEY TERM

Common land Pasture and woodland that was shared by all.

KEY DISEASE

Cholera A very infectious disease, often fatal. It is caused by poor sanitation and infected water supplies.

belief that the disease was in some way connected to Neapolitan misrule.

A lack of political debate, a police state and miserable living conditions provoked an **uprising in Palermo** on 12 January 1848. After a few days, the revolutionaries had taken control of the city and the revolution was being led by Sicilian nobleman Rosalino Pilo.

The main demand of the revolutionaries was straightforward. They wanted the re-establishment of the 1812 constitution, which had been abolished by the King of Naples in 1816. Ferdinand II would not accept the reintroduction of such a constitution, because it would have given Sicily considerable autonomy from Naples. He offered a compromise constitution, which was refused. The Sicilian revolutionaries consequently set up their own provisional government.

The nature of this government reveals much about the nature of the revolution.

- A National Guard was established to ensure that the lower orders and the more militant revolutionaries did not get out of control.
- Hostility was maintained towards Naples and all key government posts were reserved for Sicilians. The **Sicilian elections** took place in March 1848. In April 1848, the newly elected Parliament announced that Ferdinand was no longer King of Sicily. An Italian prince would be chosen as monarch in his place.
- In July 1848, the Sicilian constitution gave considerable powers to the lower house of Parliament.

This was not a radical revolution, but one that aimed at a constitutional settlement that would give Sicily its independence. However, this was not acceptable to Ferdinand and, in September 1848, he launched a military assault on the island, which earned him the nickname **'King Bomba'**. Despite the superiority in numbers of the Neapolitan army, it took them until May 1849 to finally crush the insurrection.

KEY EVENT

Uprising in Palermo, January 1848 The initial manifesto called Sicilians to rally 'to arms, sons of Sicily; our united force will be invincible'. Unfortunately it didn't mention where they might get these arms.

KEY THEME

Sicilian elections The elections to the Sicilian Parliament were open to all literate males in Sicily at the time. This did not constitute a large proportion of the population.

KEY TERM

'King Bomba' Translated from Italian, *bomba* literally means 'bomb'.

Uprising in Naples

Revolution in Sicily soon spread to the mainland. On 17 January 1848, an uprising of the secret societies in Salerno forced a series of concessions from Ferdinand, including the promise to free political prisoners. But this wasn't enough for most revolutionaries, who also wanted a constitution.

A mass demonstration in Naples on 27 January in favour of their demands forced the issue. Ferdinand agreed to grant a constitution. This was due in part to the fact that he was unable to rely on Austrian support as his father had been able to do in 1820 because, as a result of Austrian behaviour in Ferarra, **Pius IX refused to let Austrian troops cross the Papal States.**

The constitution that was issued in February 1848 turned out to be conservative in nature.

- A Parliament was to be created with an upper and lower chamber.
- The King could veto laws and could nominate members to the upper chamber of Parliament.
- A national guard was to be created, albeit under the control of the King.

The granting of a constitution in Naples raised expectation of liberals throughout the Italian peninsula. On 17 February 1848, Grand Duke Leopold granted an equally conservative constitution. In Piedmont, Charles Albert was far less willing to give in to liberal demands. However, he was finally persuaded that it would be better to give in to the limited demands of the more moderate liberals than to risk revolution and the potential of having to face more radical demands. The resulting *Statuto* of March 1848 had great significance in the coming years.

- It did not grant a full Parliamentary system. The King kept hold of important powers, including the right to sanction laws that had been passed and to appoint the members of the **upper house of Parliament**.
- However, it did create a constitutional monarchy. Parliament was given the right to introduce laws.

KEY EVENT

Pius IX refuses to let Austrian troops cross the Papal States In making his decision to deny Austrian troops access to the Papal States, Pius IX even went so far as to ask the Lord to bless *Italia*. Just the utterance of the word was enough to send nationalists into a frenzy of excitement and adulation. At this point, the papacy really did seem to have put itself at the head of the nationalist cause.

KEY TERM

Upper house of Parliament Known also as the Senate.

The **lower house of Parliament** was to be elected on a limited suffrage (only 2 per cent of the population). It was given the power to discuss financial issues.

- It guaranteed civil liberties for Piedmontese citizens such as right to religious toleration. It was in granting such liberties that the *Statuto* went further than other constitutions.

With the issuing of the *Statuto*, Pope Pius IX found it difficult to resist calls for a constitution in the Papal States. The response was limited. He allowed the creation of a Parliament, but one that had less power than those in the other states. He also denied the citizens of the Papal States the basic liberties promised by the Piedmontese *Statuto*. If contemporaries were looking, here was a clear sign of the limitations of Pius IX's liberal credentials.

Austrian refusal to respond to reform

The Austrian rulers in Lombardy refused to respond to agitation for reform. In protest, the citizens of Milan came up with an interesting way of registering their protest. The Austrian government held the monopoly over the **sale of tobacco** in Lombardy. Therefore, the form of protest taken was a healthy one. The Milanese stopped smoking.

Austrian soldiers and officers seen smoking in the streets were harassed. In itself, this boycott did not constitute a full-scale uprising. It was events in Vienna in March 1848 that were to have a considerable impact on what would happen next. The February revolution in France had inspired demonstrations in favour of reform in Vienna. As popular unrest spread, the unthinkable happened. On 13 March 1848, Metternich resigned as Foreign Minister. This was the trigger for revolution.

THE FIVE DAYS OF MILAN

On 17 March 1848, barricades were thrown up in Milan and a full-scale battle followed.

- On the one side were the Austrian governor and troops with the initial support of the city council.

What happened in the revolutions of 1848–9?

The street battle at Porta Rosa during the Milan uprising, 22 March 1848.

- On the other was a coalition of anti-Austrian forces. These included Mazzinians, liberals, around 100 priests, **artisans** and writers.

In the light of the crisis in Vienna and ferocious opposition in Milan, the Austrian commander **Field Marshal Radetzky** took the decision to withdraw his troops to the safety of the fortresses of the Quadrilateral (see page 5). The temporary collapse of Austrian rule left a political vacuum in Lombardy. The different opinions held in Milan about the future of Lombardy reflected some of the different strands of the *Risorgimento* already described.

- The more conservative moderates of the Milan City Council, led by its *podestà* Count Gabrio Cassati, feared an independent Lombard republic. Instead they proposed union with Piedmont led by Charles Albert.
- During the uprising, the more radical Milanese formed a Council of War led by Carlo Cattaneo. Their ultimate aim was the creation of a federation of Italian republics.

A provisional government was formed that was led by Cassati and dominated by the moderates. They knew that the Austrians would be back, so they asked Charles Albert for protection.

Demonstrations in Venice

It was not just in Lombardy that the Austrians were in trouble. In Venice, demonstrations took place demanding the release from prison of patriot **Daniel Manin**. The problem for the Austrians was that many sailors in the Austrian navy docked in Venice were Italian, as were many of the soldiers in the Austrian garrison in the city.

Manin was released and, on 22 March 1848, a Venetian Republic was declared. Although Manin preferred Venice to stay independent until the declaration of an Italian Republic, he accepted the vote of the newly elected Venetian assembly to also ask Charles Albert for assistance.

Piedmont declares war on Austria

At first, Charles Albert hesitated to assist. He disliked the revolutionary overtones of what had happened in Milan and Venice. However, one factor above all others convinced him that intervention was the correct course of action. At this moment of Austrian weakness and with Metternich gone, Lombardy was ripe for annexation. Other considerations that helped him to make his decision were as follows.

- He feared intervention of a military force from revolutionary France if he held back.
- He also feared that if he didn't intervene, then revolution in Milan might spread to Piedmont.

On 22 March 1848, Piedmont declared war on Austria. Its army, led in person by Charles Albert, invaded Lombardy. Charles Albert's hope was that he could annex Lombardy without a fight, because the Austrian government was in turmoil. At first it seemed that even if a battle had to be fought, then the Piedmontese stood a good chance of victory.

Troops from across Italy converged on Lombardy to join with Charles Albert to purge Italy of the hated Austrians once and for all.

- Columns of soldiers led by General Guglielmo Pepe came from Naples.

- An army led by General Giacomo Durango arrived from the Papal States.

However, Durango had exceeded his orders from Pope Pius IX, who had no wish to fight with Catholic Austria. What happened next very much shaped the course of the *Risorgimento*.

PIUS'S ALLOCUTION

For many conservative Italians, the Pope was the natural leader of Italy. Pius IX had seemingly placed himself at the head of those who wished for an Italian federation under his leadership. However, this was a misreading of Pius IX's intentions. He was not prepared to upset Catholic Austria for the sake of Italian unity. On 29 April 1848, in response to General Durango's disobedience, Pius IX issued the famous Allocution – the main points being as follows.

- Pius stated that the war against Austria did not have his blessing.
- He highlighted the fact that Charles Albert was the aggressor in the war.
- The idea of a united Italy was not one supported by the papacy and the Pope did not wish to be considered as the potential leader of any **Italian confederation**.

The Allocution shocked Italian nationalists. It also meant that Pius had ruled himself out of the leadership of Italy. The plans of the neo-Guelphs lay in tatters. From now on, the *Risorgimento* was to be tinged with anti-clericalism. From a military point of view, the Allocution weakened Charles Albert's cause as some soldiers in Durango's army would not go against the papal word. Worse was to come with the news on 15 May 1848 that Ferdinand II had re-established autocratic government in Naples. General Pepe was ordered home. He ignored his orders, but many of his troops headed south.

KEY TERM

Italian confederation
This was not to be the unified state hoped for by Italian nationalists, but a loose alliance of the kingdoms agreed at Plombières. The Pope was offered leadership in compensation for losing lands to the Kingdom of Central Italy.

THE LOSS OF LOMBARDY

Initially, Charles Albert's army was successful. In May 1848, it took Peschiera and won the Battle of Goito. However, the outlook for Charles Albert was distinctly worrying. A French army some 30,000 strong was amassing on the Piedmontese border. Within his own army he had a number of troops left over from Durango's and Pepe's armies, whom he did not trust. Even more alarming was the fact that Radetzky had persuaded the Austrian government to **fight for Lombardy** rather than give it to Charles Albert.

On 24 July 1848, the Austrian army overwhelmingly defeated the Piedmontese and their allies at the Battle of Custozza. Radetzky pressed home the advantage, the Piedmontese were expelled from Lombardy by 4 August and the **Armistice of Salasco** was brokered by 11 August.

FURTHER DEFEAT

In November 1848, Prince Felix zu Schwarzenberg was appointed Prime Minister of Austria. This move put paid to any hopes the Piedmontese might have had that the Austrians were prepared to give territorial concessions to prevent future conflict.

In Piedmont, Charles Albert was persuaded by Prime Minister Gioberti and General Domenico Chiodo (who took over as prime minister in March 1849) to try one more time to defeat the Austrians. Charles Albert hoped that victory would silence the democrats and republicans in Piedmont whose popularity had increased since the Battle of Custozza. However, the outcome was further humiliation, with Radetzky crushing the Piedmontese army at Novara on 23 March 1849.

In the wake of defeat, Charles Albert abdicated the throne of the Kingdom of Sardinia in favour of his son Victor Emmanuel II. When peace was signed in August 1849, Piedmont was forced to pay reparations of 65 million French francs. The defeat for Piedmont was a humiliating

KEY THEME

The fight for Lombardy
It was not surprising that Radetzky was keen to fight to hold on to Lombardy. He had spent most of his military career in northern Italy and understood the strategic benefits of holding the Quadrilateral. He also thought his military chances against Charles Albert's army were good. In June 1848, the Austrians ordered Radetzky to seek a negotiated peace. However, he sent Prince Felix Schwarzenberg to Vienna to persuade the government to allow him to fight, which they did.

KEY EVENT

Armistice of Salasco (1848) Named after the general who brokered the agreement. Charles Albert gave up Lombardy, although the Austrians accepted Anglo-French mediation on the understanding that it might result in territory being handed over to the Piedmontese at a later date. In reality this came to nothing.

one and was to have important short- and long-term repercussions.

- Before the first campaign against the Austrians, Charles Albert had famously claimed that Italy would *'fare da sè'* ('go it alone'). By this he meant that Italians did not need foreign help to get rid of the Austrians. Military defeat in 1848 and 1849 proved Charles Albert wrong. To defeat the Austrians militarily, Italians would need help from abroad.
- The actions of Pius IX had ended the papacy's claim to be the natural leader of Italians. From now on, Italian nationalists treated the papacy as an enemy of Italian unity.
- As the forces of constitutional monarchy and the moderate cause were defeated on the battlefield, so those with a more radical agenda took the initiative.

THE RESULT OF DEFEAT

With the defeat of Piedmont at Custozza, large numbers of General Durango's troops returned to Rome. Pius IX had issued a constitution in March 1848, but was fearful of a military *coup* and was now openly unsympathetic to the nationalist cause.

In September 1849, Pius appointed Count Pellegrino Rossi as his prime minister, hoping that Rossi would act firmly against liberal reformers and more radical democrats alike. Unfortunately for Pius, Rossi was not popular with the Rome mob and was murdered on 15 November while entering the Roman Parliament. This assassination was the trigger for insurrection against the Pope, who fled Rome on 24 November in fear of his life.

While Pius IX settled into temporary exile in Gaeta in the Kingdom of Naples, power in Rome was exercised by a revolutionary government led by **Giuseppe Galletti**. Although his government was in a difficult position with demands for reform being made from all sides, Galletti's ministry was able to introduce some popular measures in its short period in office.

- The most popular reform was the abolition of the *macinato* in January 1849.
- Also popular was the programme of public works ordered by Galletti's government. This was partly due to the large number of people employed in the building trade in Rome and the desire of the government to keep levels of employment high.
- The government proposed the meeting of a constituent assembly – the *Costituente* – to decide the future of Rome and Italy, giving responsibility for the election of the *Costituente* to a **Giunta di Stato**. It was the task of the *Giunta* to invite the election of deputies from across the whole of Italy, rather than just from Rome.

THE *COSTITUENTE* AND THE ROMAN REPUBLIC

In January 1849, elections were held in Rome. In February 1849, the *Costituente* met for the first time. Its membership was radical, although mainly middle class. Immediately it announced the end of the Pope's power and the foundation of the Roman Republic. This was not surprising given the popularity of Mazzini's ideas among many deputies in the *Costituente* and it was little surprise that Mazzini was welcomed on his arrival in Rome in March.

The rule of the radicals in Rome was not so welcomed by the Pope, nor by his allies across Europe. At a **papal meeting** with his Cardinals in April 1849, he called for foreign support to restore his power, both spiritual and temporal, in Rome. On news of the defeat of Charles Albert in March, the *Costituente* chose three people to govern Rome. Known as the triumvirate, and including Mazzini as one of the three, it was to carry on the reforming work of Galletti's government – for example, the ending of Church control of the press and the abolition of the death penalty.

Revolt in Tuscany
It wasn't just in Rome that the democrats raised the prospect of radical revolt. In Tuscany in October 1848, Grand Duke Leopold II was forced to appoint a more

'democratic' government. The new government was led by Professor Giuseppe Montanelli, who wanted a people's war against Austria. By 1849, the atmosphere had become even more radical and Leopold fled the region. However, the defeat of Piedmont forces at Novara led to the regaining of the upper hand by the 'moderates' and Leopold returned to Tuscany in April 1849.

The march on Rome

In Rome, the triumvirate was to have little time in which it could introduce reform. The Republic had few friends in Italy or further afield. Neither did it have a significant army with which it could defend itself. The clearest **threat to the survival of the Roman Republic** came from republican France.

- In France, the president, Louis Napoleon, wanted to win the support of Catholics to send a force to Italy, led by General Charles Oudinot, with orders to crush the Roman Republic.
- On 24 April 1849, Oudinot landed at Città Vecchia and marched on Rome.

The French were opposed by a makeshift force of volunteers led by perhaps the greatest hero of the *Risorgimento*, Giuseppe Garibaldi. For two months he inspired his troops to block the French army's attempt to take Rome. Meanwhile, **Mazzini's attempt to appease the French** was in the hope that they would not destroy the Roman Republic.

By June 1849, the French had amassed an army of 20,000 at the gates of Rome. Garibaldi addressed the *Costituente* promising that the future for Rome's defenders was one of 'hunger, thirst, forced marches, battles and death'. As the French entered Rome of 3 July, Garibaldi and a force of 4000 withdrew to San Marino to fight another day. Mazzini made one final appeal to the people of Rome before returning to exile in London. Without doubt the cause of Italian nationalism still fully relied on the attitude of the foreign powers.

Threat to the survival of the Roman Republic Many people in France sympathised with the cause of the Roman Republic. However, Louis Napoleon was able to win over doubters as to the wisdom of the French expedition in 1849 with the explanation that if the French didn't intervene, the Austrians would. He was also playing on the sentiments of significant Catholic opinion in France that wanted to see the Pope restored.

Mazzini's attempt to appease the French
Mazzini hoped that Louis Napoleon might have been persuaded not to attack the Roman Republic and be content with keeping an army in Italy for the purpose of deterring the Austrians from intervening. Measures taken by Mazzini included the return of French prisoners. The policy failed.

An 1849 illustration of 'Garibaldi's men'.

> **Mazzini's final appeal, 1849**
>
> In his address to the citizens of Rome in July 1849, Mazzini urged:
>
> *Romans, your city has been overcome by brute force, but your rights are neither lessened nor changed. By all you hold sacred, citizens, keep yourself uncontaminated. Let your municipalities unceasingly declare with calm firmness that they voluntarily adhere to the Republican form of government and the abolition of the **temporal power** of the Pope.*

The survival of Venice

Although Charles Albert's army was defeated by the Austrians at Novara in March 1849, the Republic of Venice survived. Thereafter the Republic, led by Daniel Manin, became a symbol of resistance against the Austrians for Italian nationalists.

The Venetian rising had little other significance. The rest of Venetia remained under Austrian control and Manin did not have a clear nationalist policy to follow. Most Venetians looked favourably on **Manin's moderation**. He reduced the taxes on important goods such as salt. He also promised universal suffrage. But he managed not to threaten the interests of the middle class or artisans with revolutionary ideas. As a result, they continued to give him their support.

Despite being besieged by the Austrian army, and despite hunger and cholera in the city, Venice held out for a year until August 1849, when Manin surrendered.

CONCLUSION

It is difficult for historians to draw conclusions from the 1848 revolutions. However, the following points can be made with some confidence.

- It is clear that the insurrections were mainly regional in nature.
- Some groups, such as the workers in Venice, hoped for revolutionary change. However, the majority were more conservative in their ambition. The confusion of aims means that it is impossible to generalise that the uprisings were either national or nationalist.
- The wars fought by Charles Albert were not wars of national liberation but an attempt to annex territory in northern Italy.
- Austrian control of parts of northern Italy and influence throughout the peninsula had been challenged but not removed.

SUMMARY QUESTIONS

1 Why did the 1848 revolutions fail?

2 What was the impact of the 1848 revolutions on the cause of Italian nationalism?

CHAPTER 5

What was the significance of political and economic developments in Piedmont 1848–59?

INTRODUCTION

In 1861 Italy was unified under Piedmontese leadership. There are a number of factors (covered in full later) that explain why this was the case. However, it is wise to start with an examination of why it was Piedmont rather than, for example, the papacy that was to play the central role in forging the new Italian state.

WHY PIEDMONT TOOK THE LEADING ROLE

The reason Piedmont took the leading role in forging political unity rather than any other of the states on the Italian peninsula lies in the nature of Piedmont's political, economic and social development after 1848.

The most important feature of Piedmont's political development after 1848 was the retaining of the *Statuto*, first granted by Charles Albert in March 1848. The fact that the *Statuto* survived in Piedmont while the liberal constitutions across the peninsula were repressed was to give Piedmont a crucial edge. From 1849 to 1861 Piedmont acted as a magnet drawing those who wished to live under a liberal constitution. Here it is worth remembering the promises made by the *Statuto*.

- Legislation would be passed by the king in Parliament – that is, with the consent of the king and two chambers (houses) of Parliament (one elected, the other nominated).
- Legislation on taxes would be introduced by the elected chamber of Parliament.

- The press would be free, albeit subject to some restraint.
- Individual liberty was guaranteed.

It is not hard to imagine the result. All of those in Italy who craved political freedom were drawn to Piedmont. In all, perhaps as many as 30,000 exiles moved north to Turin and Genoa in the 1850s. Many were intellectuals who became highly influential in public life – for example, the economist Francesco Ferrara or the writer Giuseppe Massari. Through this movement, Piedmont became the centre of Italian nationalist and liberal thought. Independent newspapers and radical journalism flourished with many writers writing from an Italian, rather than Piedmontese, perspective.

RESTRICTION OF THE POWER OF THE CHURCH

By the terms of the *Statuto*, the Catholic Church was the established Church in Piedmont. However, many of the Church's power and privileges, which had existed for hundreds of years, were considered by several Piedmontese politicians to be incompatible with various principles of the *Statuto*.

In March 1850, a member of the government, Giuseppe Siccardi, brought in a series of bills that were passed by the Piedmontese Parliament. These became known as the Siccardi Laws. The laws controlled the power of the Church. In most states this was done through agreement between Church and state known as a concordat. What made the Siccardi Laws different was that the state passed them without consulting the Church. The range of measures aimed at the Church was broad and the impact far reaching.

- Separate law courts for priests and other ecclesiastical people were abolished, because their existence conflicted with Article 5 of the *Statuto*, which stated: 'All justice emanates from the king.'
- The right of criminals to seek sanctuary and protection in churches was abolished.

- Religious groups, including monasteries, were restricted in their right to buy property.
- The number of feast days on which people were forbidden to work was reduced.

The significance of these laws should not be underestimated. They reflected the determination of Piedmont's rulers to modernise and to assert the dominance of the state over the Church. This was to be a recurring theme of the next few decades.

THE PIEDMONTESE LIBERAL STATE

One of the Piedmontese politicians who was prepared to speak out in the Chamber of Deputies in favour of the Siccardi Laws was the Minister for Trade and Agriculture, Count Camillo Cavour.

Cavour had been appointed in 1850 to the government led by Massimo d'Azeglio, which could be best described as centre-right in its political leanings. However, the Siccardi Laws marked a divergence of opinion with the more conservative right, led by Cesare Balbo and Thaon de Revel, voting against the first Siccardi Laws.

Although the centre-right did not leave D'Azeglio's government over the issue, its disapproval was clear. In December 1851, D'Azeglio attempted to appeal to those on the right by proposing a Press Law that would reduce the freedom of the press. With the Siccardi Laws also under pressure from the Pope, Cavour decided that the time was right for a realignment of Italian politics.

CONNUBIO

The left of Italian politics had been momentarily discredited with the failure of the 1848 revolutions. At the turn of 1851–2, Cavour made a Parliamentary agreement with the leader of the centre-left, Urbano Rattazzi. The result was the creation of an alliance in the centre of Italian politics know as a ***connubio***.

KEY TERM

Connubio A marriage or, in political terms, an alliance. The significance of the *connubio* should not be underestimated. It created a precedent for managing Parliamentary affairs through bribery, corruption and through forming tactical alliances. From 1871 onwards, this form of Parliamentary management was known as *trasformismo*, or transformism (see page 85).

The first consequence of the *connubio* was the clear strengthening of Parliament in relation to the Crown. In May 1852, Rattazzi was elected President of the Chamber of Deputies, despite the king's disapproval. With D'Azeglio's government weakened by the political re-alignment it was not long before his ministry collapsed. In November 1852, Cavour was asked by Victor Emmanuel to become prime minister.

As prime minister in the 1850s, Cavour was energetic in his promotion of economic change, as described on pages 53–4. However, he was also an important influence in the developing nature of the Piedmontese state and the decline in the impact of Mazzini and his followers.

ANTI-CLERICALISM

One of the most important aspects of *connubio* was the shared **anti-clericalism** of the centre left and centre right. On becoming prime minister in 1852, Cavour dropped proposals inherited from the D'Azeglio government in favour of civil marriage. However, his actions were less to do with personal conviction and due more to pressure from the king. Thereafter, Cavour was to pursue a resolutely anti-clerical line. The vast estates of their Church and their generous income of 5 million lire from the state were easy targets.

In early 1855, Cavour introduced a bill that proposed the abolition of monastic orders not involved in education or charity work. The land belonging to these orders would be taken by the state. The proposal caused a constitutional crisis; it was opposed by Senate, king and papacy. Although Cavour was forced to dilute his proposals (resulting in monks and nuns from closed monasteries receiving generous pensions), he still won, despite being forced at one stage to resign as prime minister.

In the 1857 election, the candidates of **the right** who had sympathy with the Church increased their vote. Ever the consummate Parliamentary operator, Cavour ended the *connubio* and sacked Rattazzi as Minister of the Interior.

Anti-clericalism
Throughout his political life, Cavour exhibited a strong dislike of the Church as a dominant institution. Indeed, he commented that the Catholic Church was 'the chief cause of the misfortunes of Italy'. He saw the papacy as a natural supporter of Austria. Cavour believed in religious toleration and was quite happy to be seen as the scourge of the papacy.

The right Those to the right in Italy in 1850 would be uneasy about far-reaching reform that damaged the Church. They also disliked the policies of free trade. Right-wingers feared revolution and far-reaching reforms. Those to the left, on the other hand, were more sympathetic to reform, and supported a more democratic state and the power of Parliament.

He also had to change his attitude to the Church in order to reduce the possibility of **alliances** against his government. The issue of the Church was not raised. However, Cavour's influence was important in identifying mainstream Italian politics with anti-clericalism.

THE RADICAL THREAT

One of the first issues that Cavour had to deal with was the diplomatic impact of a Mazzinian-inspired insurrection in Austrian-controlled Milan in February 1853. Not wanting to provoke any conflict, Cavour warned Austria of the impending uprising for which he received thanks from Vienna. However, his credentials as a long-term opponent of the Austrians was saved by the next move of the Austrians, which was to seize the property of citizens of Lombardy who had fled to Piedmont.

The fury this provoked distracted from the main issue, which was that Mazzini's chosen method of action had again been discredited. This was also the case in 1857, when insurrection in the Kingdom of Naples led by **Carlo Pisacane** was to end in failure. For Cavour, the added shock was that Mazzini led a simultaneous revolt in Genoa that also ended in failure.

Cavour's fury at the futility of such revolutions hid the fact that they were further proof of the unlikelihood of political change in Italy being heavily influenced by Mazzini.

THE PIEDMONTESE ECONOMY

The development of the Piedmontese economy from the mid-1840s should not be underestimated in its importance. As the introduction of the *Statuto* resulted in Piedmont enjoying a distinct political culture, so industrialisation and the building of railways in the 1850s meant that Piedmont was the first Italian region with a partly industrialised economy. As in many other parts of Europe, this industrialisation was based on the building of railways. Its impact was to further the image of Piedmont as a state in the process of modernising (as had the Siccardi Laws).

The textile industry

Piedmont's industrialisation did not solely rely on railways. A thriving textile industry based on the manufacture of wool, silk and cotton was firmly established by the mid-1840s. There were severe restrictions to the growth of industry in the north of Italy. In particular, the lack of coal hampered the development of a factory system.

Wool and silk. Both the wool and silk industries were still predominantly **domestic industries**. They were also labour intensive. The number employed in the silk industries was as high as 60,000 at some points in the 1840s.

Cotton. It was the cotton industry that dominated. Indeed, by 1844 there were approximately 114,000 cotton workers in Piedmont.

The railways

Further development of the Piedmontese cotton and other industries relied on advances in communication, most obviously the building of railways. The leading proponent of railway building in Piedmont was Cavour. His personal interest in railways would justify him being called an 'enthusiast' and even 'obsessive'.

In 1835, Cavour visited Britain to observe the construction of the London to Birmingham railway designed by **Robert Stephenson**. To Cavour, the material and political benefits of railway construction were clear. In 1845, the Piedmontese government had begun a limited programme of railway construction. In 1846, Cavour wrote an article in the French magazine *Revue Nouvelle*, which attempted to persuade Charles Albert and his ministers that large-scale railway construction would be of benefit to Piedmont. In his article, he used the following arguments.

- He said the railways were as important as the printing press.
- The railways were inevitable, and their construction in Piedmont would produce economic benefits similar to those experienced in Britain and France.
- The railways would lead to the development of a **national consciousness** and, if Piedmont was that

foremost economic power, then it would be identified more closely with a broader national interest.
- Railway construction was underway in Naples, Tuscany and Lombardy. If it was going to lead in Italian railway construction, a commitment was needed sooner rather than later.

CAVOUR'S ROLE IN PIEDMONTESE POLITICS

Cavour did not have long to wait before he was able to influence economic policy more closely.

- In October 1850, he was made Minister of Trade and Agriculture by Prime Minister D'Azeglio.
- Soon after, he was given additional responsibilities for Shipping (a post that included overseeing the operation of the Piedmontese navy), in which his scientific mind resulted in **technological improvement**.
- In April 1851, he was given the important post of Minister of Finance. He immediately undertook a reform of finances aimed at balancing the books and raising capital for large-scale projects.
- In late 1851, he borrowed heavily from the London bank of Hambro while increasing taxes.

Cavour was a firm believer in free trade and, by the end of 1851, had signed trading treaties with states including Portugal, France, Britain and Belgium. The aim of these treaties was twofold – to ensure both political support and economic growth. The reduction in tariffs resulted in a growth in trade. Between 1850 and 1859, imports and exports increased by 300 per cent.

Although Cavour became prime minister in November 1852, he did not lose interest in developing Piedmont's economy. He was also not afraid to use public money and to borrow from abroad to build new railway lines. In 1854, a significant line linking Milan, Turin, Genoa and the French border was opened. This was followed by a commitment to a number of projects, including a proposed thirteen-kilometre railway tunnel through **Mont Cenis**, which gained approval from the Italian Parliament in 1857.

KEY THEME

Technological improvement Cavour's technological mind and his interest in all things scientific can be seen in his enthusiasm for the modernisation of the navy.

- He ordered a new naval vessel from Britain powered by screw propulsion rather than paddle steam.
- He also introduced metric calibre naval guns.

Additionally, he was an agricultural innovator. On his farm in Leri, he introduced many practices widespread in Britain but less widely practised in Piedmont. These included:

- crop rotation, and
- the introduction of effective drainage.

KEY PROJECT

Mont Cenis Cavour had great enthusiasm for this scheme. In 1846, he wrote in his article in *Revue Nouvelle* that such a project would be 'the masterpiece of modern industry'.

The result was that by the end of the 1850s, approximately 850 kilometres of railway track were in operation in Piedmont. This was half the total of track laid in the whole Italian peninsula.

But it was not just the railways that grew in the 1850s. Government subsidies to a range of enterprises resulted in significant growth.

- In 1853, the electric telegraph linking Turin to Paris flourished.
- So did the textile industry, with the removal of tariffs.
- The building of canals, which began in 1857 with the construction of the Cavour canal, further boosted the construction industry.

The result of such government-driven economic modernisation was debt. By 1859, the public debt was 725 million lire. However, such a policy changed the economic status of Piedmont for good. Piedmont was now Italy's foremost industrial region with good trading links to the rest of Europe.

CONCLUSION

The 1850s were an important period of political and economic development and change in Piedmont.

- The political system and how it operated was very much conditioned by Cavour's influence and the introduction of the *connubio*.
- Economic and financial reform further enhanced Piedmont's reputation as a modernised state.
- Both political and economic change enhanced Piedmont's role as the potential natural leader of the peninsula and the power most likely to be able to expel the Austrians from Lombardy and Venice.

SUMMARY QUESTIONS

1 Describe the extent of economic change in Piedmont in the 1850s.

2 What was the significance of Cavour's role in the development of the Piedmontese political system?

CHAPTER 6

What happened on the road to unification, 1852–9?

INTRODUCTION

The foreign policy that Cavour inherited from D'Azeglio when he became prime minister was well-suited to his political viewpoint. Cavour was not an instinctive Italian nationalist. However, he found the attitude of Vienna to northern Italy unsatisfactory. In its treatment of Lombardy, Cavour felt that Austria provoked revolutionaries in and outside Italy, and encouraged reactionary and conservative forces. Despite (and also because of) the reversals of 1848–9, Piedmont foreign policy priorities remained resolutely anti-Austrian. D'Azeglio had followed a 'middle-way' foreign policy, which gave encouragement to neither Mazzinians nor **Piedmontese isolationists**, but still hoped to see Austria removed from Lombardy and Venice. Most importantly, Cavour understood that Piedmont could not dominate the north of Italy at the expense of Austria without foreign support. This was to be the cornerstone of his foreign policy.

KEY GROUP

Piedmontese isolationists
There were some within Piedmontese political circles in the 1850s such as Solaro della Margherita who believed that Piedmont as a nation would suffer through closer unity with other Italian states.

CAVOUR'S FOREIGN POLICY

Under Article 3 of the *Statuto*, foreign policy remained the prerogative of the Crown. As the king's prime minister, this gave Cavour considerable power to make foreign policy as he saw fit and without Parliament's approval. He was determined to exercise this power for the advancement of Piedmontese interests as he saw them. Primarily, these interests were:

• a weakened Austrian influence in the north of Italy, and
• the promotion of Piedmontese interests.

Victor Emmanuel II (left), Cavour (centre) and Garibaldi (right). These three men were jointly responsible for the concept of Italian unification.

In 1854, Britain and France declared war against Russia and sent troops to fight in **the Crimea**. In January 1855, Cavour decided to join the war on the side of the allies (Britain and France). He ordered the despatch of 15,000 troops to the Crimea. Cavour took this decision for a number of reasons.

The Austrian position. Austria remained neutral throughout the war. However, it was clear that by late 1854, Russian antagonism towards Austria was increasing. In November/December 1854, it signed a Four Points agreement with Britain and France aimed at forcing Russia to the negotiating table by the end of the year. For Austria to have acquired such a powerful enemy as Russia was a diplomatic benefit for Piedmont. But Austria's close understanding with Britain and France worried Cavour.

The British and French position. The military force that Britain and France sent to the Crimea in 1854 was ravaged by cholera. It was therefore very clear to both countries that they would need reinforcements. By mid-1854, the

KEY PLACE

The Crimea A peninsula in south Ukraine. The main cause of war here was tension between Turkey and Russia over Russian demands for greater influence in parts of the Ottoman Empire. This included demands for control of the Holy Sites in Palestine and the role of protector of Christians within the Ottoman Empire.

British and French governments placed pressure on Piedmont to join the war.

The position of Victor Emmanuel II. Victor Emmanuel welcomed the pressure placed on Piedmont. By the beginning of 1855, the king had signified that he was prepared to appoint a more pro-war prime minister such as Count Thaon de Revel because of **Cavour's reluctance for war in 1855.** Indeed, it became known to Cavour that the king had entered into private negotiations with the French.

WAR AND PEACE

The Piedmontese troops arrived in the Crimea in the early summer of 1854. Many troops were soon struck down with the cholera that had decimated the British army in particular. However, the Piedmontese army did not disgrace itself taking part in the victory over the Russians at Chernaya Rechka on 16 August, which led directly to the fall of Sebastopol.

The number of Piedmontese soldiers killed that day, fourteen, does not quite back up the claim of a famous victory. But the battle won the Piedmontese army the respect and gratitude of its allies. In December 1855, Austria threatened to enter the war on the side of the allies and the Russians sued for peace. At the Congress of Paris of February to April 1856, neither Britain nor France was prepared to alienate Austria by addressing any Piedmontese request for a change in the *status quo* in the north of Italy. However, Cavour did achieve a number of points.

- His attendance at the Congress was a sign of Piedmont's growing diplomatic stature.
- Although Italy was not mentioned until peace had been signed, the 'Italian Question' was the main topic of discussion on 8 April. This was an important step on the road to recognition that Austrian domination of northern Italy was a diplomatic issue.
- The French and British were grateful to Piedmont for its support. This fact would be crucial if and when Piedmont were to militarily challenge Austrian rule.

KEY THEME

Cavour's reluctance for war 1855 Cavour's reluctance for war reflected the mood of many in Piedmont who opposed the idea of war against Russia when the real enemy was deemed to be Austria. Others, such as cabinet member General Vittorio Dabormida, opposed going to war without first receiving firm promises of support from the allies.

CAVOUR AND THE NATIONAL SOCIETY

Foreign support and diplomacy are often highlighted as the main successes of Cavour. However, his cultivation of the National Society was of crucial importance.

Formed in the mid-1850s, the membership of the National Society was dominated by Italian exiles living in Piedmont. The aim of the society was to promote the cause of Italian unity. At some time or another, many of its members had supported Mazzini. But by the 1850s, the leaders of the society **Giorgio Pallavicino** and Giuseppe La Farina, plus converts such as Daniel Manin, were prepared to accept that unification might come under the leadership of Piedmontese monarchy rather than as a republic.

In 1856, Manin and Cavour met. At this point, Cavour was still sceptical of unification. But despite the two men not agreeing on the future of Italy, their meeting was another stepping stone on the road to change. In the same year, Cavour met the adventurer Giuseppe Garibaldi to discuss the possibility of war with Austria. Such contacts and the role played by the National Society became very important in later years.

THE SUPPORT OF LOUIS NAPOLEON III

Cavour understood that French support for the removal of Austria would best serve Piedmont's interests. In Napoleon III, he and Piedmont had a potential useful ally, as the following factors show.

- As a 22 year-old, Louis Napoleon had taken part in the uprising in Rome in 1831 and conspiracies in the Papal States and Modena. Such enthusiasm for the romantic notion of Italian liberty and nationalism was to last throughout his political life.
- Napoleon was grateful to Piedmont for support during the Crimean War and built a close working relationship with Cavour. After the Congress of Paris in 1856, a dialogue was maintained through intermediaries that

included Napoleon's nephew Prince Jerome and Cavour's trusted assistant Costantino Niagra.

However Napoleon did not act solely with Italian interests in mind.

KEY AREA

Nice The issue of the status of Nice was particularly sensitive. It was feared that if news of the potential transfer of Nice's ownership to France became public it would split opinion in national-minded circles. Most importantly, it would alienate the adventurer, soldier and patriot Guiseppe Garibaldi, who was born in Nice.

- As the inheritor of the Bonapartist title, he saw it as his duty to ensure the expansion of France. In particular, he saw the possibility of expanding into **Nice** and Savoy (which were part of the Kingdom of Sardinia) in return for help to expel the Austrians from northern Italy.
- It is possible to interpret Napoleon's help for the cause of Italian unity as being less inspired by romantic ideals and more the hope that, through helping Piedmont assert itself in northern Italy, France would create a client state that would allow it greater influence in that region.
- Napoleon was always wary of Catholic opinion in France. In 1849, he sent French troops to Rome to help crush the Mazzinian-inspired rising and restore the papacy. This move went down well with the Catholics in France. Napoleon never wavered from his commitment to protect the Pope, a commitment that prevented the full unification of Italy until 1871.
- It is also likely that Napoleon envisaged a federation with the Pope at its head rather than the creation of a centralised Italian state. How this would work can be seen in the planning at Plombières (see pages 60–61). There is also little doubt that Napoleon hoped to further the dynastic interests of family members through engineering their appointment to kingdoms in central and southern Italy.

NAPOLEON AND PLOMBIÈRES

The attempt on Napoleon's life

On 14 January 1858, four Italians, led by Count Felice Orsini, attempted to assassinate Napoleon as he arrived at the opera with his wife, Empress Eugénie. The rationale for such action was that the **assassination of Napoleon** would lead to the restoration of a republic in France that would be well disposed to the creation of an Italian republic. In the event, Orsini's bomb failed to harm its

KEY EVENT

Attempted assassination of Napoleon In January 1858, an attempt was made to assassinate Louis Napoleon III. The instigator of the attempt, Orsini, hatched his plans in London, where three large bombs had been made for him. Then he travelled by train to Paris with three co-conspirators (two Mazzinians and a hired assassin). Following a tip-off, the *gendarmarie* (French police) had been expecting Orsini and his co-conspirators to arrive from England by road. However, the would-be assassins outwitted them by arriving via Brussels.

target; it did, however, manage to kill seven onlookers and injure 150 others.

At his trial, Orsini appealed to Napoleon to actively support the cause of Italian unity. By doing so, he would ensure that 'the blessings of 25 million citizens would follow him to posterity'. It has been assumed that these words in some way created a spark in Napoleon's conscience that triggered him into action and led to the arrangement of a meeting in Plombières on 20 July 1858. This assumption is dubious. Napoleon might have wanted to use Orsini's plea as a romantic cover for what was, in reality, some hard-nosed bargaining.

- Napoleon wished to ensure that there were no further attempts to assassinate him. Therefore, he saw a meeting with Cavour as a way of putting pressure on him to introduce repressive measures against violent nationalists living in Piedmont.
- Napoleon saw this as a chance to deal with a dynastic problem – the difficulties he had had as leader of the Bonaparte family in finding a wife (and role in European affairs) for his cousin, Prince Jerome Bonaparte.
- Both Cavour and Napoleon wished for **war against Austria**. A potential problem was that their motives for war differed. Cavour wanted war to remove Austrian influence from northern Italy. Napoleon wanted war to gain territory but also as part of a broader diplomatic strategy regarding Austria.

France's and Piedmont's agreement at Plombières

It was agreed at the secret meeting in Plombières that France would join Piedmont in war against Austria, if war could be provoked in a way acceptable to opinion in the two countries. The aim, of course, was to use military force to drive Austria out of Italy. Other terms of the agreement were as follows.

- A Kingdom of Upper Italy (ruled by the House of Savoy) would be created to cover the provinces of Piedmont, Lombardy and Venetia, and the duchies of Parma, Modena and the Papal Legations.

KEY THEME

War against Austria It was suggested by the historian A.J.P. Taylor in an article in the *English Historical Review* in 1936 that Napoleon might well have wanted to wage war with Austria as a means of improving diplomatic relations. He points to the fact that there had been an improvement in relations between France and Russia after the Crimean War, and that Napoleon saw no reason why this might not be the case after a war with Austria.

- A Kingdom of Central Italy would be controlled by Tuscany, and would also include Umbria and the Papal Marches.
- Rome and the surrounding area would remain in the control of the papacy and the Pope would lead an Italian confederation.
- For the present time, the Kingdom of Naples would remain as it was. This was mainly because Napoleon feared that to unseat the Bourbons might upset the tsar, who saw himself as an ally of this similarly autocratic dynasty.
- In return for the support of 200,000 French troops, Napoleon demanded Savoy and Nice. Cavour was quite happy to accede to the request for Savoy, the majority of its population being French speaking. However, this was not the case in Nice and it took until January 1859 for Piedmont to agree.
- More important for Napoleon, the agreement was to be sealed with the marriage of the fifteen year-old Marie Clotilde (daughter of the Italian king, Victor Emmanuel II) to the middle-aged **Prince Jerome Bonaparte**.

WAR WITH AUSTRIA, 1859

The problem for Cavour was how to provoke war with Austria in such a way that the reality of his and France's ambitions were not too obvious. In his opening of Parliament on 12 December 1859, **Victor Emmanuel** delivered a deliberately provocative **speech**, but to little effect. This was the least of Piedmont's worries.

1858–9

At Plombières, Cavour had promised to match Napoleon's promise of an army of 200,000 with a force of 100,000. However, by the turn of 1858–9 this was proving hard to find. The National Society recruited some 20,000 volunteers, but many of these men were untrained and no match for the Austrian army. The army reserves Cavour hoped to mobilise did not exist. In the end, the Piedmontese army numbered around 60,000.

KEY PERSON

Prince Jerome Bonaparte (1784–1860) A rather gentle and slow member of the Bonaparte family, Jerome had little energy or charm. His family nickname, 'Plon-plon', sums up his character rather well. When the wedding took place between 'Plon-plon' and Marie Clotilde on the eve of conflict with Austria in 1859, she was quickly labelled the first casualty of the war.

KEY IDEA

Victor Emmanuel's speech In his speech, he threatened: 'For while we respect treaties we are not insensitive to the cry of anguish that reaches us from so many parts of Italy'.

- There was no popular enthusiasm for war. In 1848–9, war against Austria was seen by many as a popular crusade. This time, though, things were very different, the war being engineered by Cavour.
- When an insurrection began in the Duchy of Modena, it failed through lack of support. The nature of this campaign against Austria, one organised through diplomacy rather than encouraged from below, was clear to see.
- Indeed, Cavour was worried that Austrian rule in Lombardy under Archduke Maximilian was not as repressive or unpopular as it had been.
- A war in northern Italy was unpopular with other European powers. The Prussians made it clear that their sympathies would be with Austria, although the Russians had assured France of their neutrality and goodwill. In Britain, the prime minister, Lord Derby, and his foreign secretary, Lord Malmesbury, were sympathetic to the cause of Italian unity, but did not wish to see a war deliberately provoked. To many, Austrian domination in northern Italy would be replaced by French domination, which was equally undesirable. They pressed for a Congress of European powers to resolve the issue. To Cavour's horror, it seemed that Napoleon was increasingly convinced of the desirability of a peaceful solution to the Italian question.

However, as the diplomatic manoeuvrings continued, so tension increased.

March to June 1859

In March 1859, the Piedmontese army was mobilised. The Austrians followed suit in April. The problem for the Austrians was that, having mobilised, they now needed to either use their army or demobilise, which would be costly.

Therefore, on 23 April the Austrians demanded Piedmontese demobilisation within three days. When it was not forthcoming they declared war and, on 29 April, troops under General Franz Gyulai invaded Piedmont. However, the Austrian army was delayed by poor weather, which gave the French plenty of time to move their army by rail into Piedmont.

In April 1859, in Florence there was a popular demonstration against the Grand Duke Leopold that resulted in his flight and the creation of a provisional government led by **Baron Bettino Ricasoli** that favoured union with Piedmont.

In May 1859, the National Society engineered peaceful revolutions in Tuscany, Modena and Parma, and the rulers of all three fled leaving provisional governments in control.

In June 1859, the Duke of Modena and the Duchess-Regent of Parma fled their provinces. They were replaced by a government led by **Luigi Farini**, which was, again, close to Piedmont. Indeed, government under Farini was akin to being ruled as a Piedmontese colony, because all major governmental decisions were approved in Turin.

There was further political unrest when, in June, insurrections took place in the **Papal Legations**. In Bologna (the capital of the Papal Legations), Piedmontese commissioners moved in to restore government. Most of these commissioners were members of the National Society. Only in Tuscany was there any demonstration of popular support for a change in government.

In 1859, unlike 1848, change was manipulated from above, the main agent of this manipulation being the National Society. However, the political future of these provinces relied, in the short term, on events on the battlefield.

The battles

Minor victories by the Piedmontese army at Palestro and by Garibaldi's *Cacciatori delle Alpi* at Como in May 1859 helped to pave the way for the two large-scale battles of the war at **Magenta** (4 June) **and Solferino** (24 June).

The Austrians were defeated at both battles, but the margin of victory for the French and Piedmontese was narrow. The Austrians still held the Quadrilateral and showed no sign of withdrawing from northern Italy. Indeed, there was little prospect of the French and

Painting of Napoleon III at Solferino, 1859, by Beauce. The picture shows the carnage on the battlefield.

Piedmontese defeating the 150,000-strong Austrian army, which was well entrenched without considerable bloodshed.

NAPOLEON'S ATTEMPT AT PEACE

Napoleon's ambition to have freed Italy 'from the Alps to the Adriatic' seemed unlikely to be fulfilled in the short term. So, without Cavour knowing, he sued for peace with Austria.

- An armistice was proposed by Napoleon on 8 July 1859.
- This was followed by a meeting at Villafranca on 11 July between Napoleon and the Emperor Franz Joseph. Apart from his distaste for the bloodshed, Napoleon had other motives for making peace behind Piedmontese backs.

Revolution in central Italy. Napoleon disapproved of the turn of events in central Italy. He felt that the papacy was under threat with a National Society government-friendly to Piedmont in Bologna. He also felt that Piedmontese control of central Italy went beyond the points agreed at Plombières. Napoleon was embarrassed by the demands of French Catholics for him to act to rectify a situation that was clearly getting out of hand.

Lord Palmerston (1784–1865) Palmerston originally became a Tory Member of Parliament in 1807. He joined the Liberals in 1830, and was prime minister from 1855 to 1858, then again from 1859 to 1865. Palmerston made it known that he was anti-Austria south of the Alps (that is, in Italy), but pro-Austria north of the Alps.

Lord John Russell (1792–1878) Russell first became a Member of Parliament in 1813. He was prime minister from 1846 to 1852. He became Lord Palmerston's foreign secretary in 1859. Russell was a strong supporter of Italian unification, as were most Liberals at the time. He was also a believer in free trade and argued that a free, united Italy would be a strong trading partner for Britain. His belief that the Italian Question should be solved by applying the idea of self-determination was echoed by the President of the United States of America, Woodrow Wilson, at the end of the First World War some 60 years later.

Prussia Prussia was willing to support Austria as long as it was allowed greater influence among the organisation of German states known as the German Confederation.

Napoleon I and the coalition By the end of the Napoleonic Wars in 1815, Napoleon I faced a coalition that included Britain, Prussia, Austria and Russia.

Foreign disapproval. In the middle of June 1859, a new Liberal government was formed in Britain with **Lord Palmerston** as prime minister and **Lord John Russell** as Foreign Secretary. Both men were sympathetic to the cause of Italian unification. However, they were restrained by domestic considerations (including the views of Queen Victoria) and maintained a policy of strict neutrality. The government in **Prussia** made it known that it might lend some support to Austria by mobilising its armies along the River Rhine, thereby threatening France. The outline of a **coalition** as faced occasionally by his uncle (**Napoleon I**) was becoming ominously clear to Napoleon III and was to be avoided at all costs.

VILLAFRANCA

At Villafranca, Piedmont's ambitions were forced to play second fiddle to the diplomacy of Napoleon. Some aspects of Plombières survived, but many did not.

- Austria agreed that Lombardy should be given to France, which might then choose to give it to Piedmont in due course. However, Venetia was to remain in Austrian hands.
- Piedmont was not to be given control of Modena or Parma and the rulers who had been forced to flee from the central Italian states were to be restored. Piedmont was also forbidden to annex Mantua and Peschiera in Lombardy.
- An Italian confederation was to be set as up, as agreed at Plombières, with the Pope at its head.

The effect on Cavour was predictable. He resigned his post as prime minister and was not present at the signing of the Treaty of Zurich in November 1859, which formally ended the war. As part of the treaty, Napoleon suggested that the issue of central Europe be decided by a Congress of the European powers. This was a compromise that did not please the Piedmontese government, now led by Alfonso Lamarmora.

The following labels appear on the map:

AUSTRIA–HUNGARY

SWITZERLAND

Border of Italy

Other national border

Regional borders

Battle and date

SAVOY
(to France)
1860

LOMBARDY
1859

VENETIA
1866

Magenta
(1859)

Solferino
(1859)

Custozza
(1866)

PIEDMONT

PARMA
1860

MODENA
1860

OTTOMAN
EMPIRE

DALMATIA

NICE
(to France)
1860

ROMAGNA
1860

SAN MARINO
(Independent Republic)

Castelfidardo
(1860)

MONACO
(Sardinia 1815–60.
France 1861)

Florence
(capital 1864–71)

MARCHES
1860

Adriatic Sea

Lissa
(1866,
Austrians destroy
Italian fleet)

TUSCANY
1860

PAPAL
STATES

Lagosta

CORSICA
(French)

Elba

THE PATRIMONY
1870

Mentana
(Garibaldi, 1867)

Rome
(1870,
capital 1871)

Gaeta
1861

Benevento
(Papal,
1860)

(Garibaldi,
1860)

Naples

NAPLES

Tyrrhenian
Sea

SARDINIA

SARDINIA (PIEDMONT)

KINGDOM
OF THE
TWO
SICILIES
1860

Mediterranean Sea

Palermo
(Garibaldi, 1860)

Aspromante
(Garibaldi, 1862)

0   50   100   200 miles

0   30   60   90   120 km

SICILY

N

TUNISIA

KINGDOM OF SARDINIA

The unification of Italy, 1859–70.

TURNING POINTS ON THE ROAD TO UNIFICATION

Despite agreeing at Villafranca that the rulers of the central
Italian states should be restored, Napoleon accepted later
in the year that the decline in the Pope's temporal power
was inevitable. In December 1859, a pamphlet written on
behalf of Napoleon and entitled *The Pope and the Congress*
was published in Paris. In it, Napoleon suggested that he

would be prepared to accept that the Pope should lose control over the Legations. This was the crucial turning point on the road to unification. By accepting a decline in papal power, Napoleon upset Catholics in France and the Austrians. But he very much pleased the British.

The main consequence of the pamphlet was that the idea of the Congress was dead. It was the British foreign secretary Lord John Russell who seized the moment. He proposed that the future of the Italian peninsula should be decided through the application of the principle of **self-determination**. This was another crucial moment. Cavour returned as prime minister on 21 January 1860 and immediately negotiated a deal with Napoleon.

- Piedmont would hand over **Savoy and Nice** to France.
- France would accept Piedmontese annexation of the central Italian duchies, as long as the annexation was accompanied by plebiscites (popular votes).

PIEDMONTESE ANNEXATION

In a sense, Piedmontese annexation of the central Italian states had a certain inevitability about it. Despite Villafranca, Grand Duke Leopold did not return to power in Tuscany. Instead, power was held by Baron Ricasoli, who had engineered the election of a subservient local assembly, which, in August 1859, had voted to ask for annexation by Piedmont.

Meanwhile, Ricasoli exercised power as a dictator. In **Emilia**, Farini had remained equally powerful. The plebiscites were an opportunity for them to engineer annexation with the help of the National Society, which campaigned enthusiastically. All males over 21 were given an opportunity to vote. Their choice was:

- annexation to the constitutional monarchy of Victor Emmanuel II, or
- a separate kingdom (the nature of the 'separate kingdom' remaining deliberately vague).

KEY TERM

Self-determination When a group of people decide their own political destiny and status.

KEY AREA

Savoy and Nice The British strongly objected to the French having Savoy and Nice. To Lord Palmerston and Lord John Russell it was the first step towards the creation of a new Bonapartist empire. One must remember that Napoleon I's attempts to create a European empire had been defeated only 45 years earlier.

KEY PLACE

Emilia In 1859–60, this term referred to Modena, Parma, the Papal Legations and Bologna.

When the elections took place in March 1860, it was clear that there was widespread vote rigging. It was little surprise that the plebiscites resulted in a crushing victory for those in favour of annexation. The votes were as follows.

	For annexation	Against annexation
Tuscany	386,445	14,925
Emilia	427,512	756
Savoy (to France)	130,583	235
Nice	24,448	160

There was not much doubt that the **plebiscites** were a charade, that Cavour's government had hidden behind the cloak of popular suffrage. In reality, the annexations were the result of the diplomacy and the skills of the National Society and the Piedmontese commissioners in the central Italian states.

FROM ANNEXATION TO UNIFICATION

What happened next was to turn the annexation of central Italy by Piedmont into the unification of the peninsula. The reaction of Garibaldi to the surrender of his birthplace, Nice, to the French was to organise a force to prevent its annexation. The group that became known as '**The Thousand**' met near the port of Genoa. As the group increased its numbers, news broke in April 1860 of an insurrection on the island of Sicily. Although about only one-tenth of Garibaldi's force were Sicilian, he was persuaded by two of his most trusted followers, **Francesco Crispi** and Rosalino Pilo, to sail south. Garibaldi concurred. On 12 April, Pilo sailed on ahead to rally the Sicilian revolutionaries and inform them that help was close at hand.

Cavour, Garibaldi and liberation
Once at sea, Garibaldi declared that he was going to liberate Italy in the name of 'Italy and Victor Emmanuel'. The Mazzinians among The Thousand were reluctant to give their allegiance to a monarchy, but this reluctance was tempered by Mazzini's acceptance in March 1860 of

KEY THEME

Plebiscites The voting figures from the plebiscites are so one-sided that the historian Martin Clark wrote in *The Italian Risorgimento* (1998): 'Hitler and Stalin in their heyday never received results like this.'

KEY GROUP

The Thousand There were actually more than 1000 volunteers who rallied behind Garibaldi. More than half the force were from Lombardy. Many were students with a few professionals and workers involved. Several volunteers wore red shirts to symbolise their willingness to spill blood in the name of Italy – hence their nickname 'Garibaldi's Red Shirts'.

KEY PERSON

Francesco Crispi (1819–1901) Crispi had taken part in the uprising in Sicily in 1848 and thereafter went into exile. He returned in 1860 to join Garibaldi's expedition to Sicily. He became a politician in the new state and was elected to be a deputy in the Italian parliament in 1861. Crispi was twice Prime Minister of Italy, from 1887–91 and 1893–6, and became one of the most significant prime ministers of the new Italian state.

An 1863 painting by Borrani entitled 'The Sewing of Red Shirts'. The picture shows a group of women preparing shirts to be worn by the volunteers of Garibaldi's army, otherwise known as The Thousand.

Victor Emmanuel as leader of a united Italy if that was the popular choice. As Garibaldi headed south, so Cavour was faced with a difficult dilemma.

- To oppose Garibaldi would make his government unpopular at home and would offend the members of the National Society, which had recently so admirably served the Piedmontese cause in central Italy.
- Cavour suspected that Victor Emmanuel supported Garibaldi's escapade.
- Elections were due to be held on 6 and 10 of May, and Cavour did not wish the issue of Garibaldi to damage his political prospects in any way.

On 11 May 1860, **Garibaldi landed in Sicily** but met little opposition. The ranks of The Thousand were swelled with new Sicilian recruits as they marched on Palermo. The key to what happened next was military competence. Garibaldi's Thousand may well have been poorly armed with dated muskets. However, they were well trained.

KEY EVENT

Garibaldi lands in Sicily
For a short while Garibaldi acted as ruler of Sicily, which was no easy task. At first he sought to please the peasants by abolishing the grist tax, a tax on milling corn. However, widespread unrest led him to use force to restore law and order to the relief of the nobility.

Garibaldi was a first-rate military commander who was surrounded by a small group of similarly experienced soldiers.

The first encounter with the Neapolitan army at Calatafimi on 15 May resulted in a sensational victory for Garibaldi's troops. Palermo was taken later in the month. The island of Sicily was conquered by the end of July.

Cavour panicked and sent his **agent, Giuseppe La Farina**, to Sicily to claim its annexation to Piedmont. However, Garibaldi was not quite ready to hand over his hard-fought gains just yet and La Farina was sent away empty-handed. A more acceptable envoy, Agostino Depretis, was despatched instead. None the less, he failed to stop Garibaldi embarking for the mainland on 19 August.

Cavour's and Garibaldi's opposition and sympathisers

For Cavour the danger was that the situation was developing out of his control. At this stage, he still did not envisage a unified Italy including the south. Even more worrying for Cavour was that Garibaldi might initially aim to invade Naples, although he knew that his ultimate target was Rome. But any threatening of Rome would result in opposition from the French, and Cavour realised that any resulting conflict would end in a French victory.

The British, however, were sympathetic to Garibaldi's expedition, and the crossing of the Straits of Messina was undertaken under the watchful and sympathetic eye of the Royal Navy. Those wishing to stop Garibaldi now attempted to act, but their efforts were too little too late.

- Cavour ordered Admiral Persano of the Piedmontese navy to sail to Naples and organise a pro-Piedmont insurrection before Garibaldi arrived in the city. He failed. In the face of Garibaldi's success, Cavour had to reassess his attitude to the whole episode.
- The ruler of Naples, Francesco II, formed a liberal ministry in late June 1860 and restored the 1848 constitution in early July. He failed to convince his

subjects that his political conversion was authentic.
As Garibaldi's army made its **invasion of Naples**,
Ferdinand and his court fled north to Gaeta.

Garibaldi in Naples and Cavour's reaction

In early September 1860, Garibaldi's army took Naples
and planned to defeat Ferdinand's army, which had
withdrawn to the north of his kingdom. As Garibaldi
planned his invasion of the Papal States, Cavour acted.
The National Society engineered an uprising in the Papal
States on 8 September. Cavour demanded that the papal
army be disbanded rather than suppress the uprising.

**Garibaldi's campaigns
and expeditions during
1860.**

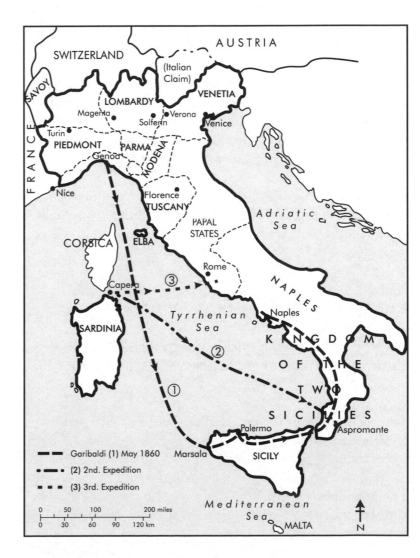

The problem for Cavour was that the uprising was a damp squib, and a number of powerful voices inside Piedmont (for example, D'Azeglio) and abroad (for example, the governments of Spain and Portugal) complained that Cavour was acting in breach of international law. However, he ignored such protests and the Piedmontese army invaded the Papal States from the north on 11 September 1860. Napoleon was aware of the invasion and did not object as long as the Piedmontese army avoided Rome.

On 18 September, the papal army was destroyed at the Battle of Castelfidaro. However, the Neapolitan army was still intact. Garibaldi's task was to defeat this army, thereby opening the way to a convergence of forces fighting in the name of Victor Emmanuel II. Victory was achieved on 26 October 1860 at the Battle of Volturno.

Meanwhile, plebiscites were arranged in the south with the simple question: 'One Italy, Victor Emmanuel: yes or no?' The result was not surprising, although enthusiasm for the Piedmontese king was limited. Most Sicilians and Neapolitans were voting for the end of the feudal monarchy of the Bourbon family.

The voting figures for the plebiscites held on 21 October were as follows.

	Yes	No
Sicily	432,053	667
Naples	1,302,064	10,312

These were followed by plebiscites arranged in the more northerly provinces of the Marches and Umbria that were held in November 1860.

The voting figures for these ballots held in November 1860 were as follows.

	Yes	No
The Marches	133,765	1212
Umbria	97,040	360

The relationship between Garibaldi and Victor Emmanuel

From 3 October 1860, the Piedmontese army was led in person by Victor Emmanuel. On 26 October, Garibaldi and Victor Emmanuel met at the head of the two armies at Teano. A triumphal entry of Naples was stage-managed on 7 November, and **Garibaldi** formally handed his conquests over to **the king**. Thereafter, Garibaldi was politically isolated despite the fact he had just completed the conquest of nearly half of the Italian peninsula in the name of the Piedmontese king!

In Piedmont, Garibaldi was not portrayed as a hero but as an illiberal, authoritarian figure. Indeed, he helped to encourage this image by asking for special powers to rule the south for another year. These were refused. So he left for his island home of Caprera promising, rather ominously for Victor Emmanuel, to return to free Rome and Venice, which were still in foreign hands.

KEY THEME

Garibaldi and the king
Despite entering Naples together in triumph in November 1860, the two parted on bad terms. The king refused to inspect Garibaldi's army of Red Shirts, despite their loyalty. In return, Garibaldi refused titles and pensions. He opted instead for a year's supply of macaroni as a reward.

FOREIGN REACTION TO UNITY

Few of the foreign powers showed great enthusiasm for recent developments. A meeting of the rulers of Austria, Prussia and Russia in Warsaw in October 1860 received the news of Piedmontese expansion coolly. It was even suggested that the Austrians might invade Lombardy while Piedmontese forces were engaged elsewhere. Although this plan came to nothing, it reveals the diplomatic tension surrounding the expansion of Piedmontese influence.

The reaction of the British government of Lord Palmerston was entirely different. Not only did the British welcome Italian unity, but also the foreign secretary Lord John Russell made a public announcement to that effect on 27 October to the delight of Cavour. Even better, the British government warned that 'if any other power' should attempt to intervene to prevent Italian unity, the British government would intervene militarily to prevent such action.

CONCLUSION

Italy had been unified through a number of factors.

- The impact of foreign powers should not be underestimated.
- Nor should the diplomacy of Cavour and his use of the National Society be overlooked.
- Garibaldi's importance was in shaping the unification of Italy as one of the whole peninsula, not just the north.

SUMMARY QUESTIONS

1 How significant was the role of France in the unification process?

2 Explain the importance of Garibaldi in influencing the shape of the new Italian state.

CHAPTER 7

What happened on the road to unity, 1861–71?

INTRODUCTION

The unification of Italy in 1861 was, in reality, Piedmontisation. The constitution of that year imposed the legal structures, political institutions, foreign policy and cultural norms of Piedmont on the rest of Italy. In January 1861, elections were held for the Parliament of the new Italian kingdom and the constitution adopted in March 1861 was based on the Piedmontese *Statuto* of 1848.

- Symbolically, the king, Victor Emmanuel, remained 'the Second' (as he was of Piedmont) rather than 'the First' (as of the new state).
- As a constitutional monarchy, the sovereign body of the state would be the king in Parliament.
- The Chamber of Deputies of the Parliament was elected on a minimal suffrage of approximately 2 per cent of the population.
- The state's administrative structure was centralised. At a local level, prefects (who were often from the north) wielded considerable power and influence in the name of the Crown.
- Piedmontese taxes, weights and measures and, most important, the idea of free trade were imposed on the rest of Italy.

From the start, the problem for the new Italian state was clear. How was it to reconcile the new state, its institutions, laws and customs to large areas of Italy which found those new institutions, laws and customs to be alien? In his book *Modern Italy 1871–1995* (1996), historian Martin Clark explains the chasm between what he terms 'legal Italy' (that is, the state) and 'real Italy' (those who were not part of the new 'legal Italy'). Many Italians felt

An engraving entitled 'The Liberators of Italy'. Among others, the illustration includes Admiral Persano (top row, second left), Rattazzi (middle row, second left) and General Orsini (bottom row, third from left).

isolated and betrayed by the imposition of a centralised state that was essentially Piedmont writ large. Therefore, the new pattern of government of Italy that was to dominate for many decades to come was set. The unification of Italy had been from above. 'Legal Italy' would attempt to absorb those who wished to be reconciled. Those groups that did not would be repressed.

THE SOUTH

Many Piedmontese politicians, including Cavour, had very little understanding of **the south**. Its poverty, backwardness and distinct economy meant it was unsuitable for a unification with Piedmont based on Piedmontese laws.

An illustration of incompatibility can be seen in primary school education. In 1859, the Piedmontese Parliament introduced a law insisting on two years' compulsory education. However, the vast majority of the population of the south were illiterate. In Sicily and Naples, Garibaldi's invasion had caused the peasantry to expect a better standard of living. Both areas had a long tradition of regional autonomy. Indeed, in the early summer of 1860 Cavour let it be known that he was considering some form of 'real self-government' for the southern regions after annexation to Piedmont.

But 'real-self government' never materialised. Cavour's immediate aim in October 1860 was to crush any

KEY PLACE

The south Cavour was untypical of many Piedmontese politicians in that he had visited Florence. However, he had never been as far south as Rome, let alone Naples. The first Italian prime minister to visit the south was Giuseppe Zanardelli, who toured Calabria in September 1902. He died a year later, which many of his contemporaries thought proof of the dangers of going south.

opposition in the south, whether it be from those still loyal to the Bourbons, the remnants of Garibaldi's army, peasants demanding land or those hoping for some freedom. Cavour despatched Farini to the south with orders to crush opposition militarily.

Officers of the Bourbon army were treated rather well. In fact, by the start of 1861, 2000 or more had been given commissions in the Piedmontese army. However, the foot soldiers fled to the safety of the mountains as the Piedmontese General Enrico Cialdini ordered that all those found carrying weapons be shot.

New taxes were introduced by the Piedmontese state to reduce the 2.5 billion lire of national debt accumulated during the recent wars. The result was the re-emergence of brigandage and a war, the **Brigands** War, which was fought with great brutality and claimed more lives than the wars of unification. Civil liberties were suppressed in the south and the Piedmontese deployed an army some 120,000 strong to deal with the threat.

LOMBARDY AND TUSCANY

It was not just in the south that Piedmontese rule was imposed. However, Piedmontese rule was implemented at a different pace in different regions.

Lombardy. While Cavour was out of office in late 1859, Piedmont acquired responsibility for governing Lombardy. The Minister of the Interior, Rattazzi, decided that the best course for the state was to impose a central model of government on both Lombardy and Emilia, despite the fact that Lombardy had been promised a Constituent Assembly to discuss the issue at the time of the plebiscite. The problem was, there was no common language. (Only 2 per cent of Italians spoke the language; all others spoke dialect.) Lombardy had its own education system, legal system and structure of local government. These were swept away by Piedmontisation.

Tuscany. In Tuscany, the imposition of Piedmontese laws was delayed for political reasons. The powerful Baron Ricasoli argued successfully for the protection of Tuscan customs and legal systems, at least in the short term. However, Tuscany was the exception rather than the rule. In most regions, the local ruling class were not able to negotiate with Piedmont from a position of strength.

CAVOUR'S ELECTION VICTORY AND HIS OPPOSITION

The election of January 1861 resulted in a significant victory for Cavour's centre right group, which was now called *La Destra* and which dominated government until 1876. In opposition were the following groups.

- The centre left, led by Rattazzi and Depretis.
- The far left, which included Garibaldians, democrats from Tuscany and those who argued for a federal state.
- The far right of around twenty deputies, some of whom hoped for the restoration of the old order, the others simply being reactionaries.

In April 1861, Garibaldi appeared in the Chamber of Deputies, furious at the treatment of soldiers from his red-shirted army. His main complaint related to the treatment of his 7000 officers, who had not been incorporated into the Piedmontese army as Garibaldi had hoped. He attacked Cavour for wanting to start a civil war in 1860. Cavour denied the accusation.

Cavour also had to face the opposition to his government from the Church. Because of the loss of two-thirds of its land to the new state, the Catholic Church refused to recognise the state's existence. Cavour hoped to persuade the Church to give up Rome and its temporal power. In return he could offer it freedom of action. In March 1861, he made a speech promising 'a free Church in a free State'. However, the Church was unresponsive to Cavour's suggestions.

In June 1861, Count Camillo Cavour died of **malaria**.

KEY DISEASE

Malaria An often fatal fever that is carried and passed on by mosquitos.

CAVOUR'S SUCCESSOR

Cavour's successor was Baron Ricasoli. However, the baron lacked Parliamentary experience and was succeeded as prime minister by Urbano Rattazzi.

- Both prime ministers attempted to emulate Cavour by forming governments with the centre-left and centre-right represented.
- Unlike Cavour, neither objected to Garibaldi's continuing agitation for the seizure of Rome.

'Roma o morte' 'Rome, or death!'

In early 1862, Garibaldi set up the Society for the Emancipation of Italy. In June 1862, he left his self-imposed exile and sailed for Sicily with the tacit support of Victor Emmanuel and Rattazzi. After rallying the Sicilians with the cry of '**Roma o morte**', he crossed to the mainland.

Rattazzi was faced with alienating the French and therefore sent a military force to block Garibaldi's advance. At Aspromonte, Garibaldi's army surrendered to the Piedmontese. They were pardoned soon after. Rattazzi was sacked, but his successors were to be weakened by the combination of a lack of full support from the king and weak Parliamentary discipline.

THE ISSUES OF ROME AND VENICE

The issues of Rome and Venice remained unresolved.

Rome. At a convention in September 1864, Napoleon agreed to evacuate Rome within two years in return for the switch of Italian capital from Turin to Florence. Indeed, when the Italian government (led by Marco Minghetti) agreed, Napoleon believed that the Italians had given up their claim on Rome. This was not the case. There was a storm of protest in Italy.

- Twenty-three people were killed during rioting in Turin.
- Piedmontese deputies withdrew support from Minghetti's government.

- In his usual subtle style, Victor Emmanuel sacked Minghetti for not keeping him fully informed.

Venice. The issue of Venice was resolved through more direct and traditional means – the use of diplomacy and war. The architects of change were Napoleon and the Prussian Chancellor Otto von Bismarck. In his desire for Prussian domination of Germany, Bismarck embarked on a complex diplomatic campaign to win support for an intended war against Austria. At Biarritz in October 1865, he met Napoleon, who promised neutrality in any forthcoming war. Napoleon also helped to broker an alliance between Bismarck and Italy, then signed a secret treaty with Austria, both of which were potentially beneficial to Italy.

- The alliance between Prussia and Italy was completed in April 1866. By the terms of the alliance, Italy was to receive Venice for supporting Prussia in a war if it broke out in the next three months. To the disappointment of some Italian nationalists, Prime Minister Lamarmora failed to secure the region of Trentino as part of the agreement.
- The secret treaty between Napoleon and Austria was signed in June 1866. Austria promised to give Venice to Napoleon in return for French neutrality in the coming war.

'Resolution' of the Venice issue

On 20 June 1866, the Italians declared war on Austria. Confidence was high. It had an army of 40,000, which was far larger than the Austrian army. However, the Italians were ill-prepared and were defeated at the Battle of Custozza. Some days later, on 3 July, the Austrians were crushed by the Prussians at Sadowa.

The Austrians were forced to cede Venice to France, who promptly handed it over to the Italians. The manner in which the Italians gained control over Venice was seen as humiliating. The humiliation was made worse by a crushing **defeat at sea** at the hands of the Austrian fleet near Lissa on 20 July 1866. Although Venice was won, the Italian military and state were brought into some disrepute

KEY EVENT

Defeat at sea The Battle of Lissa was one of the first battles between 'ironclad' ships. Although the Italian navy had a greater number of ships than the Austrians, the Italian commander Admiral Persano was particularly incompetent and the Austrians found little difficulty in outwitting the Italians.

A lithograph of the Battle of Lissa by Josef Puttner. The illustration shows the defeat of the Italians to the Austrian fleet.

in the process. The plebiscite held in Venice to approve annexation was even more one-sided than usual, with 642,000 voting in favour and only 69 voting against.

OUTSTANDING NATIONAL ISSUES

KEY THEMES

Roman Question The status of Rome and the papacy's control over it.

Theological matters The most important theological matter concerning Pope Pius IX was the issue of the Virgin Mary's immaculate conception. This matter was concluded in 1854 with the proclamation of the Dogma of the Immaculate Conception.

Syllabus of Errors In the *Syllabus of Errors*, the Pope's rejection of liberalism could not have been more clear: 'It is an error to believe that the Roman Pontiff can and ought to reconcile himself to and agree with progress, liberalism and contemporary civilisation.'

With the acquisition of Venice, the outstanding national issues were the position of the Church in Italy and the **Roman Question**. After the crushing of the 1849 revolution, Pope Pius IX paid more attention to **theological matters** and left matters of state to his secretary of state, Cardinal Antonelli. It was Antonelli who framed the papal letter *Quanta Cura* with the added *Syllabus of Errors* issued in Pius IX's name in 1864. The *Syllabus* was a gauntlet of defiance thrown down by the Pope to the new social and political order in Italy.

- In the *Syllabus*, Pius rejected most of the philosophies developed in the nineteenth century from communism to nationalism and liberalism to rationalism.
- He claimed for the Church control over the education system and, therefore, all culture and science.
- The Catholic Church rejected the idea of tolerance for other religions.
- The Church asserted the idea of the continuing temporal power of the papacy.

The publication provoked an outburst of anti-clericalism from enemies of the Church, but also disappointment among the more liberal Catholics who had hoped that Pius IX was still capable of modernising the Church.

The focus of the Church

The new Italian state surpassed monastic orders and forced the Church to increase taxation payments to the state. In 1866, a law was passed demanding that most religious orders should hand over all property to the state.

The tension between Church and state reflected the declining temporal power of the Church and an important shift in its priorities. From now on, the Church was to focus more heavily on its spiritual role. This was shown in the next important move made by Pius IX. In 1869, a **Vatican Council** met. The main business of the Council was to agree with the dogma of papal infallibility – that is, that the Pope's pronouncements were indisputable. When the dogma was proclaimed in July 1870, it marked the spiritual supremacy of the Pope.

Impact on Rome

The increase in spiritual dominance of the papacy by 1870 was in direct contrast to the collapse of its temporal power. For Italian nationalists, Italy was not complete without Rome as its capital. In December 1866, the last French troops left Rome as promised in 1864. Garibaldi again attempted to seize the moment. In October 1867, he hoped that a spontaneous uprising in Rome would lead to the collapse of papal power.

However, such an uprising was not forthcoming, with many Roman citizens staying stubbornly loyal to papal rule. Instead, Garibaldi's invasion provoked the French into sending troops back to Rome. This was not to be taken lightly; the French army now had the new breech-loading chassepot rifle.

At the Battle of Mentana on 3 November 1867, Garibaldi's troops were mown down. The failure of the Italian government led by Rattazzi to prevent the humiliation of those attempting to liberate Rome led to its

The Vatican Council This met from December 1869 to October 1870. It was the first general council of the Church's bishops since the Council of Trent three centuries before.

fall. The failure of the citizens of Rome to rise in the cause of liberation led many Catholics to argue with justification that Rome did not wish to be part of a united Italy.

Rome becomes part of Italy

Rome eventually became part of Italy in a similar way to Venice. Bismarck's desire to unite German states under the leadership of Prussia led him to provoke **war with France** in 1870. Victor Emmanuel's instincts were to support Napoleon, but his government insisted on neutrality.

As the Prussian army threatened French borders, so French troops departed from Rome leaving it defenceless again. In September 1870, the French army suffered a crushing defeat at Sedan. The government of Lanza seized the opportunity to take Rome. There was little enthusiasm among the Romans for such an invasion, despite resounding support in the plebiscite held in the city on 2 October that showed 133,681 of the Eternal City's citizens approved of annexation to Italy while only 1507 objected.

Rome was pronounced the capital of the new Italy. The Church proclaimed its opposition and Pius IX declared himself to be a 'prisoner in the Vatican'.

CONCLUSION

The unification of Italy did not come about through popular uprising or even with the consent of the people (despite the plebiscites which are unreliable as indicators of popular opinion). The following factors had more of an influence.

- Again, as stated at the end of Chapter 6, the role of foreign powers was crucial, especially France. Without foreign support and the course of events working in Italy's favour, it is difficult to see how the nation state would have been built.
- The relative decline of Austria is a very important factor. Before 1848, Austrian dominance of Italian politics made nationalist aspirations difficult to fulfil. As Austria declined, so its role as a brake on change was reduced.

KEY EVENT

War with France War came as a result of an argument over who would become King of Spain. Bismarck engineered the proposal of a Prussian candidate, Prince Leopold. France objected to this proposal, fearing an ally of Prussia the other side of the Pyrenees. Diplomatic activity ended with a demand by the French for the withdrawal of Leopold as a candidate and a determination on the part of the French to humiliate Prussia. Bismarck engineered an increase in tension, revising a report of a meeting between the French and Prussians at Ems to make it sound as if war was inevitable. On 19 July 1870, the French declared war.

- The political and economic strength of Piedmont meant that it was in a position to dominate the peninsula. Unification came not from below but from above.
- Piedmontese military force, the work of the National Society and the support of strategically important and influential groups in the Italian regions resulted in a political settlement that was, in effect, Piedmontisation.
- The series of events resulted in the unification of the whole of Italy rather than a smaller state in the north.
- One should not ignore the role of individuals such as Cavour and Garibaldi.

SUMMARY QUESTIONS

1 How significant was the role played by Germany and France in shaping the development of the Italian nation between 1861 and 1871?

2 To what extent can it be claimed that the new state was 'structured on a basis of Piedmontisation'?

CHAPTER 8

Postscript: 1871 onwards

INTRODUCTION

The development of the Italian state after 1871 is crucial in giving the historian insight into how unification took place. In particular, 'legal' Italy in all its forms did little to actively integrate real Italy into the political or economic system. The limitations of social policy and social discontent reflected in unrest and large-scale emigration underline this point.

The process of *trasformismo* was basically one of bribery and corruption, and was the successor of Cavour's system of *connubio*. Its aim was to achieve the maintenance of power of the ruling elites. It went hand in hand with repression for those groups not absorbed. It is very difficult in this sense, or in any others, to claim with conviction that Italy was, in fact, truly unified by 1914. Indeed, it is possible to argue that the years 1871 to 1914 not only highlighted divisions in Italian life, but also saw the accentuation of them.

From the start, there were those who lay outside the state, most importantly the Catholics did not vote because of the papal opposition to the new state. Those elected tended to be local dignitaries and usually members of the liberal establishment. Local government was controlled by centrally appointed 'prefects', whose job was to control the municipal councils (*commune*) and the mayors who ran them.

TRASFORMISMO

The Chamber of Deputies was managed by the prime minister of the day by granting them favours. There was no party system; it was more a loosely defined 'left' (mainly associated with the south of the country) and a loosely defined 'right' (associated with the North).

- Governments came and went with regularity. There were 28 from 1871 to 1892. The same was not true of ministers, though. Agostino Depretis, for example, held the post of prime minister for all but two years between 1876 and 1887 despite numerous governments.
- As governments were essentially non-ideological and lacking a coherent doctrine, policy was implemented in piecemeal fashion.
- The governments of the right, which dominated until 1876, were characterised by public order and low expenditure policies.
- From 1876 to 1887, governments were dominated by the so-called left and the *trasformismo* of Depretis. In 1882, the suffrage was widened to 7 per cent of the electorate, but this was partly to favour the left. Certain reforms were undertaken, such as compulsory primary education in 1877 and the abolition of the grist tax on milling in 1883. The periodic governments from 1887 to 1896 of Francesco Crispi introduced reforms that widened the local suffrage in 1889 by 2 million and gave large councils the chance to elect their own mayors. A new tariff was imposed in 1887 on imported goods to protect northern industrial and agricultural interests. This had important consequences, as discussed on pages 89–90.

FOREIGN POLICY

As a new state, successive governments consciously followed a cautious line abroad.

- In 1882, Italy joined the Triple Alliance with Germany and the Habsburg Empire.
- In 1885, it began its own colonial expansion by the seizure of the port of Massawa.
- In 1890, Crispi joined up Italy's East African colonies to form Eritrea. This had been preceded in the 1880s by a vast expansion in Italy's naval capacity.

None of this was to match in importance the effects of the defeat of Italian forces by the Abyssinians at the **Battle of Adowa** in 1896. The shadow of colonial failure cast itself into the next century.

Battle of Adowa (1896)
Never had a European power been comprehensively defeated by an African army. The legacy of Adowa as an unprecedented humiliation should not be underestimated.

HEINEMANN ADVANCED HISTORY

OPPOSITION FROM THE CHURCH

The early years after unification saw opposition to the state come from many quarters. Most significant was the hostility of the Catholic Church. By the *Syllabus of Errors* of Pope Pius IX of 1864, the Church denied the validity of the new state's claim to legitimacy. From then onwards, the state often passed legislation that was anti-clerical.

- The Law of Guarantees of 1871 gave the Crown a veto over the appointment of bishops. Further legislation disbanded religious orders and banned pilgrimages. The Roman Question remained unresolved. Hence, from March 1871, Catholics were advised not to vote in elections.
- In 1886, **Pope Leo XIII** went further and banned Catholics from voting. There was little respite in the tension between Church and state.
- In 1890, Prime Minister Crispi reformed the country's charity-based welfare system to exclude the Church. This was a major blow to the Church's position in society.
- *Rerum Novarum*, the papal response of 1891, set out the principles for a form of 'Social Catholicism' – that is, that Catholics had a role to play in intervening in the economic sphere to alleviate the effects of exploitation. This was backed by the reorganisation from 1892 to 1894 of the major Catholic lay movement, the *Opera dei Congressi*, as an organisation that could implement these ideas.
- The response of the government to this perceived threat was a crackdown in 1897 on Catholic associations. A year later, all Catholic organisations were crushed. From then on, the state and Catholics were drawn closer together in informal alliances against what was seen as a far more serious threat to both.

The issue of reconciliation of Catholics to the state was partially aided by the disbanding of the *Opera dei Congressi* in 1905. The replacement lay movements, such as the *Unione Donne Cattoliche* for Catholic women, continued the strong influence of the Church. There was some participation of Catholics in elections from 1909 and Catholic-dominated local governments in towns throughout Italy – in particular in Lombardy and Venetia.

The Roman Question was still unresolved at the beginning of the First World War (1914).

OPPOSITION AND REPRESSION

Anarchism spread rapidly in the early years of the new nation.

- In 1874, there was an attempted armed rising in Bologna and another failure at Matese three years later.
- Repression against anarchists in 1878–9 followed an attempt on King Humbert's life in 1878.
- Many anarchists were forced into exile, but King Humbert was assassinated by an anarchist in 1900.
- The development of organised socialism was perceived as a far more serious threat to the liberal establishment in the long term. The 1880s saw repression of emerging movements such as the *Partito Operaio Italiano* (POI).
- In 1884, the revolutionary socialist party *Partito Socialista Rivoluzionario di Italiano* (PSRI) was founded. It was led by Andrea Costa. Most significantly, the workers' congress convened in Genoa in 1892 formed the intellectual basis of the *Partito Socialista Italiano* (PSI), founded in 1895 as an evolutionary Marxist party and led by Filippo Turati. In its organisation and structure it was a modern European party, which attracted 216,000 votes in the 1900 election. As with other groups outside the liberal establishment, the socialist movement suffered periodic repression – for example, in October 1894 the PSI was dissolved and its deputies arrested. The **Chambers of Labour**, which were worker self-help organisations, were closed down in the repression of 1897.

RADICALS AND REPUBLICANS

In the tradition of Mazzini, Italian Republicanism flourished after 1871 – especially through the medium of workers' aid societies. Many republicans supported **irredentism**. Periodically, the movement was repressed (such as the arrest of leaders in 1874).

Italian Radicals were led by Garibaldi in the 1870s, but absorbed into the government of the left. The 1880s saw the movement challenge imperialism, yet also challenge itself by the growth of workers' parties. In the 1890s, the Radicals came to the fore with a comprehensive political programme of institutional reform, regional autonomy, civil rights and social legislation based on the Pact of Rome of 1890.

Fear of such ideas and the growth of parties that stood outside the establishment prompted a constitutional debate in the 1890s based on the politician Sidney Sonnino's article in 1897 in which he said it was time to 'return to the *Statuto*' – that is, to greater executive power. These ideas were discredited in the Parliamentary wrangling of 1889–1900, and the election of 1900 ushered in a victory for the left, Socialists, Republicans and Radicals with 96 seats.

ECONOMIC DIVISION

Perhaps the greatest division within the Italian state was the economic chasm between north and south. The contrast between a capitalist north (with its large farms, irrigation and technical improvements) and the feudal south (blighted with malaria and sub-division of land) did not change as a consequence of unification. Indeed, unification reinforced and accentuated the division.

The sale of Church land after 1861 (500,000 acres between 1867 and 1874) resulted in the consolidation of the economic and political power of the local elites. It was found to be the case that this class had also benefited from the decline of the feudal system and the auction of common land. Therefore, the process of land redistribution reflected the balance of political power and reinforced the feeling of alienation, which manifested itself in the *fasci* (see page 92) of Sicily, for example.

The tariff of 1887 is further proof of the close relationship between political and economic elites. In 1886–7, nearly 1 million tonnes of cheap wheat were imported, mainly from the USA. Those who were hit hardest were large wheat-growing landowners, and the Corn Laws – which raised import duties from 14 lire/tonne in 1887 to 75 lire/tonne by 1894 – were in the interests of that class. The reciprocal tariffs imposed by France and other European countries after 1887 hit the southern agricultural economy of wine and olives particularly hard (wine production fell by around 25 per cent from 1886 to 1890).

AGRICULTURAL REVOLUTION

The '**agricultural revolution**' was limited to the north, in particular around the Po Valley.

- While wheat production in the north grew by 100 per cent from 1873 to 1913, in the south the amount of land cultivating wheat actually fell by 8 per cent between 1883 and 1913.
- The state heavily invested in land reclamation. But the bigger picture is of northern progress and southern stagnation. Of the 352,000 hectares improved by 1915, only 2300 were in the south.
- The massive emigration discussed below was a clear indicator of the imbalance of the state's intervention in the agricultural sector. Its priority in the south was to cultivate and maintain the support of local elites. Hence, subsidy and legislation were framed in a way that ensured continuity. In 1906/7, laws relating to Calabria were passed granting tax concessions on land, monies for construction projects and agricultural credit.
- Any attempt at real reform (such as Sonnino's proposed land and social reforms of 1906 to create a literate land-owning peasantry in the south) were opposed with great hostility by the southern establishment and were not implemented.

The consequence was geographical economic division and social unrest.

EMIGRATION

The real test of a united Italy is the extent to which the state had managed to 'make Italians' out of a

---

KEY TERM

'Agricultural revolution'
This was based on machinery, innovation and capital investment.

---

geographically, linguistically and culturally divided population in 1871. As with the political and economic structures, certain national institutions had developed but social division predominated. The most obvious manifestation of this fact was the **increase in emigration** from Italy in the period.

Increase in emigration In fact, the whole issue of emigration was one used by new writers such as the nationalist Gabriele d'Annunzio, who saw it as a reflection of the failure of the liberal establishment to make Italians.

- In 1879, roughly 20,000 Italians emigrated to America. By the turn of the century, the figures were much higher (see Section 6, page 145).
- Although this period also saw increasing internal migration (especially into the northern industrial cities such as Milan, whose population doubled between 1901 and 1911), much of the migration into cities was from the hinterland. In fact, only 12 per cent of the workers of the northern provinces counted in the 1911 census were born outside their province.
- The figures show that the transatlantic migration was predominantly southern (70 per cent). This is not surprising when the crippling effects of the 1887 tariff are considered.
- Although many northerners emigrated to northern Europe to find work, this migration was more seasonal. The fact is that Italy permanently lost over 1.5 million citizens between around 1900 and 1914, and most of these were from the south.

LANGUAGE

A major obstacle to 'making Italians' was the linguistic differences of the peninsula. It was not that most Italians did not speak 'Italian', but that the vast majority spoke in dialect. It was only in Rome and parts of Tuscany (the birthplace of the modern language) that Italian was commonly spoken (that is, by 2.5 per cent of a population of around 26 million).

This continued to be the case as the state lacked the will and resources to promote widespread education reform and, through it, literacy, which would have familiarised Italians with their new mother tongue. Yet, to an extent, this was intentional. As we have seen, the illiterate were deliberately excluded from the political process by the restricted suffrage. In reality, this effectively excluded much of the population of the south. It is likely that around 70 per cent were illiterate in 1871 – a figure that had fallen to just under 40 per cent by 1911. In the province of Calabria, however, illiteracy stayed at around 70 per cent of the population in 1911, while in Piedmont it fell to 11 per cent.

RIOTS AND UNREST

Periodic riots threatened political stability. Most important was the food rioting of 1898 in response to high food prices and protection on imported wheat. Riots, many of which turned into demonstrations for greater political liberty, took place across the country. The demonstrations in Milan in May ended in violent repression with perhaps up to 150 people killed. The rise of the *fasci* posed a further challenge to the establishment. Manifesting themselves in different guises, these groups were rural-based and loosely socialist in their ideals. Highly complex in organisation, the *fasci* were involved in rural strikes, which provoked their banning in 1894 by Crispi's government.

GREATER STABILITY POST-1900

The period from 1896 to 1914 saw rapid economic growth, in particular in the industrialising north. Considering the significant boom in the economy post-1900, it is not surprising that Italy was politically far more stable. There was further integration of at least sections of groups such as the Catholics and Socialists into the liberal system. The main architect of this process from 1903 to 1914 was **Giovanni Giolitti**. It was achieved by a series of concessions to appease different political groups.

- In 1902, the Supreme Council of Labour was set up to advise on labour issues and legislation as a concession to the labour movement.

KEY GROUP

Fasci The *fasci* were organised groups who aimed to improve the lives of peasants and (in urban areas) artisans and workers. The term 'fasci' derived from the Latin word 'fasces' which referred to a bundle of rods worn as a symbol of authority before Roman magistrates.

KEY PERSON

Giovanni Giolitti (1842–1928) The ultimate manipulator of the political system. He was prime minister on and off from 1903 to 1912. He was also a central political figure during the First World War and in the dying years of the Liberal State after 1918. His skill was his ability to balance the support of groups that might not see eye to eye in broad coalitions.

- **Radicals** were brought into government.
- Despite Giolitti's attempts to reduce government intervention in trades disputes and strikes, there was still considerable public disorder as shown by the general strike of 1904, called in response to the shooting of a striking miner in Buggeru.
- There were some improvements in social welfare. For example, in 1902 legislation limited the working day for women to eleven hours and in 1907, a rest day in the week was made compulsory.

THE LIBYAN WAR

The emerging threat for Giolitti and the 'liberal establishment' was **Italian nationalism**. The conservatism of Giolitti and the concessions towards socialism offended the middle classes, and these grievances were aired at the first Nationalist Congress in 1910. To an extent, the invasion of Libya in 1912 was an attempt to conciliate nationalist opinion. The Libyan War was victorious, but became the catalyst for the collapse of the system.

- The socialist PSI, on whom Giolitti had relied for support, was split by its opposition to the war.
- The nationalists won support for the war and in 1913 won five seats in Parliament.
- Most importantly, the war had strengthened the case for universal suffrage. In 1912, all literate men over 21 and all illiterate men over 30 were given the vote.

The results of the 1913 election seemingly backed the introduction of wider suffrage – the Liberal and 'constitutional' seats. In other words, all the votes Giolitti could count on fell, but only to 318 out of 511. Much more disconcerting for liberal politicians was the rise of mass politics. Under the 'Gentiloni Pact', Liberal candidates (perhaps more than 200) who agreed to sign the seven points of the Catholic Electoral Union received the Catholic vote. The crucial result was that the Liberal system relied on Catholic support.

In 1913, a major strike in Turin was won by the Socialist engineering union *Federazione Italiana Operai Metallurgici*

(FIOM), with many industrialists blaming Giolitti and his policy of non-intervention. By the eve of the First World War, the Giolittian system had crumbled with the tension of balancing the support of such disparate groups as Radicals and Catholics.

CONCLUSION

The Liberal State survived (virtually) until 1914. However, the nature of unification (Piedmontisation, for example) had a serious impact on how the state developed between 1871 and 1914.

- The new Italian state was based on a narrow suffrage, and the political system operated through the use of corruption and repression.
- The failure to reconcile Church and state distorted the development of the Italian state. In particular, the failure of Catholics to vote in national elections until 1909 meant that the political system lacked a conservative party that might have given it balance.
- Unification did not solve the economic divisions of north and south. In many cases it made them worse. Mass emigration reflected the alienation felt by many.
- The period saw some foreign policy success, but that success was overshadowed by the impact of a few disasters.

SUMMARY QUESTIONS

1 What evidence is there from the 1871–1914 period to back the claim that 'Italian unification not only failed to solve the divisions within Italy but made them worse'?

2 'The Italian state ruled through a mixture of repression and absorption.' To what extent do you agree with this statement?

AS ASSESSMENT

INTRODUCTION

This section is for those studying Edexcel Unit 2 *The Road to Unification, Italy c. 1848–70* and OCR Unit 3 *Italy 1830–70*. The structure of questions for both examination boards is similar. Here are a number of examples of the types of questions asked.

Type a
These questions ask candidates to demonstrate knowledge and understanding of key factors.

Example 1. Explain the economic and political factors that contributed to Piedmont's influence in Italy by 1860.

Example 2. Examine the importance of foreign powers to the unification process in Italy between 1854 and 1860.

Example 3. Identify and explain the different aims and objectives of Italian nationalists in the period 1830–48.

Type b
These questions relate to the comparison of the relative importance of different factors.

Example 4. Compare the importance of Cavour and Garibaldi in the unification of Italy in 1860.

Example 5. Compare the importance of at least three different factors in the unification of Italy.

Example 6. Why did the revolutions of 1848–9 fail?

Type c
These are causal questions.

Example 7. Why did the cause of Italian nationalism fail in Italy in 1848–9?

Example 8. Why was Italy unified under a monarchy in 1861?

Example 9. Why did Venice and Rome become part of the Italian state by 1871?

Type d

These are explanation questions.

Example 10. In what ways did Louis Napoleon advance the cause of a unified Italy?

Example 11. Describe the measures taken by Austria between 1848 and 1860 to prevent the advance of the cause of Italian unity.

Example 12. Describe the influence of Mazzinian nationalism on the process of Italian unification to 1860.

HOW TO GIVE THE BEST ANSWERS

The twelve questions above and on page 95 seemingly ask for different skills.

- Some ask candidates to explain.
- Others ask candidates to weigh up a number of factors.
- There are some questions that ask candidates to prioritise factors.
- Others ask for explicit analysis.

In reality the skills needed to answer these questions are similar.

The key to examination success is technique. To reach the top level, candidates are expected to show good examination practice. Below and on page 97 is a series of tips to help you answer AS questions for either examination board.

Focus on the question. Before starting your answer it is critical that you work out the focus of the question. Your answer must be written in direct response to that focus.

Argument. Although it seems that some questions do not ask you to argue, this is misleading. To achieve top level in all questions you must develop a line of argument in your response that you sustain from the beginning to the end of your answer.

Explanation. The points of argument that you make in response to the question should always be thought through and explained fully.

Evidence. This is crucial to the quality of your response. You should back up the points you make with accurate and intelligently chosen evidence – facts, dates, detail.

Without specific examples to prove your point you will not be able to achieve the highest levels.

Linkage. At AS level it is absolutely critical that you link factors together. This can be done at the beginning and the end of each paragraph. The links need to be fully explained rather than simply stated.

A couple of tips

Plan. Before you start writing you must plan your answer, even if you only have a couple of minutes to do so. The main element of the plan is the lines of argument you are going to follow. When you have written these out in the form of four or five bullet points you are ready to start writing. Use the points in the plan as your introduction and follow them through your answer.

Paragraph length. At AS level you do not have much time to write. Therefore your paragraphs should be short, snappy and to the point. Use them to identify the different factors of your argument.

EXAMPLE ANSWER

Below is an example of an answer to example question 9.

> Why did Venice and Rome become part of the Italian state by 1871?

In her answer, the candidate has attempted to identify what she sees as the most important factor. She has also attempted to explain the link between the two factors of the rise of Prussia and the decline of French power. This is an example of a very successful answer that was awarded a top mark.

The most important factor in explaining why Venice and Rome were part of Italy by 1871 is the rise in the military power of Prussia and the diplomatic skill of its minister-president Bismarck. The exclusion of Venice and Rome from Italy in 1861 had relied on the power and influence of Austria and France. Both were humiliated by Prussia and Italy was to benefit. This was partly because Bismarck used Italy in alliance against Austria; in 1866 the two countries signed an alliance that promised Venice to Italy in the event of war. However, it was not so much the event of war that was the deciding factor but the crushing defeat of Austria at the hands of the Prussian army at Sadowa in 1866. That Bismarck did not see Venice or Italy as crucial to Prussia's plans was lucky for Italy, especially because Italian forces were heavily beaten by the Austrians at Custozza and Lissa. Italy would also benefit greatly from Prussian aggression in 1870 when Prussian forces crushed France leaving Rome a free city. So Prussian aggression should be seen as a crucial factor.

However, such aggression should not be seen in isolation. The changing priorities of Louis Napoleon are heavily linked to the growth in the Prussian threat, especially after 1867 and the defeat of Austria. Until that time Louis Napoleon guaranteed the papal rule of Rome, as can be seen in the intervention of French troops against Garibaldi in 1867. Although Louis Napoleon had promised to remove French troops by the September Convention of 1864, it was only with the growing threat of Prussia that his protection of Rome lapsed. When, in 1870, Prussia invaded France, Italy stayed neutral because politicians such as Prime Minister Lanza recognised that war against Prussia was unwise. So the influence of Prussia on France and Italy at this stage was important.

REMINDERS

- Plan your essays.
- Focus on the question.
- Create an argument.
- Write in short paragraphs.
- Explain your argument.
- Back your ideas up with relevant detail.

Below are two examples of plans that help to answer the questions in examples 8 and 10.

Why was Italy unified under a monarchy in 1861?

Key points
- Italy was unified under a monarchy because of the economic power and diplomatic status of Piedmont.
- Mazzinian democracy was not a realistic alternative. The actions of the papacy resulted in the withdrawal of the pope from the role of natural leader of the papacy.

In what ways did Louis Napoleon advance the cause of a unified Italy?

Key points
- Louis Napoleon's role should not be underestimated, in particular in providing the military force with which Austria was expelled from Lombardy.
- Louis Napoleon also provided the diplomatic support for Italian unification.
- However, one should not exaggerate the extent of Louis Napoleon's impact – his policies acted as an obstacle to the unification process when considering Rome.

A2 SECTION: ANALYSIS AND INTERPRETATION

INTRODUCTION

This section of the book offers a more analytical examination of the principal questions concerning the *Risorgimento* and the political unification of Italy. It attempts to give key points of analysis to the reader and examines some of the points of argument put forward by the leading historians of the subject. It is hoped that the points of analysis will inform the arguments of AS and A2 students when they are debating or writing about Italian history of the period in question. The areas of debate covered are as follows.

- **Section 1: What was the impact of Mazzini and the failure of 1848–9?** This section looks at the nature of Mazzinian nationalism, and how it stood both as an inspiration and as a threat to other Italian leaders.
- **Section 2: What were the roles played by Cavour and Garibaldi in the unification of Italy?** Here the impact of Cavour on the *Risorgimento* is examined, as is the significance of Garibaldi. This section contains an in-depth analysis of the critically important events of 1859–60.
- **Section 3: What led to the failure of the Church, 1848–71?** The role of the Church as a political force is examined closely, as is the part it played in dictating the course of unification. Particular attention is paid to the role played by Pope Pius IX and the true nature of his papacy.
- **Section 4: What was the role and impact of foreign powers?** The focus here is on the role of foreign powers in the unification process. In particular, the section examines the diplomacy of the 1850s and 1860s, and the diplomatic priorities of the leading European states when dealing with Italy.
- **Section 5: What were the significant economic, social and cultural divisions in Italy in the period 1848–71?** A number of factors hindered the political unification of Italy, most obviously economic, cultural and social divisions. This section assesses the significance of these divisions and judges how far they were healed by 1871.
- **Section 6: What were the strengths and limitations of a united Italy in 1871 and beyond?** The nature of unification of Italy in 1871 was to influence the political, economic and social development of the state thereafter. This section looks at the extent to which Italy was truly unified in 1871 and beyond.

SECTION 1

What was the impact of Mazzini and the failure of 1848–9?

KEY POINTS

- The *Risorgimento* was, primarily, a cultural movement. At its heart was the aim of a socially narrow group of Italians to promote an Italian cultural reawakening in Italy. Those associated with the *Risorgimento* aimed to promote the idea of national consciousness and the ideal of closer political unity, most obviously at the expense of the Austrians.
- At the heart of the political element of the *Risorgimento* as an ideal was Guiseppe Mazzini.
- Mazzini's vision of democracy threatened those in power. Therefore his ideal of national unity was hijacked and distorted by those in Italy who wished to see it as a means of justifying their political action.

THE *RISORGIMENTO* AND HIGH POLITICS

The question often asked is: To what extent did the *Risorgimento* shape the unified Italian state? In the popular culture of post-1871, Italy was represented by films such as *The Taking of Rome* (made at the end of the nineteenth century). Here, the *Risorgimento* was portrayed as a flourishing of patriotism, resulting in the defeat of Italy's enemies and the achievement of unification. However, such a view of the *Risorgimento* should be challenged. There were a number of insurrections in this period, although few were inspired by the *Risorgimento*. The unification of Italy was not a product of revolution or mass action, but a result of the actions of those we might term the powers of **High Politics**.

Throughout the nineteenth century in Italy (as elsewhere), the preoccupation of the forces of High Politics was to restrain the growing influence of Low Politics. One should define Low Politics as the politics of the masses, of democracy and of Parliament. Italy was not unified through the actions of Low Politics. Neither did the new Italy of 1861 reflect the hopes and expectations of the people. The *Risorgimento* was not a movement of Low Politics. Its appeal was limited, because it represented the cultural expression of an elite. Therefore, for example, the operas of Verdi in the early 1840s inspired the Milanese nationalist middle class. The 'Chorus of the Hebrew Slaves' in *Nabucco* (1842) was written to represent the enslavement of the Italian peoples. But Verdi's

> ### KEY TERM
>
> **High Politics** The establishment, kings, rulers, military leaders, judiciary and Church.

interpretation was not typical of the view of the majority of those who lived on the Italian peninsula and even those who lived in Lombardy. It should be remembered that, in 1848, the Lombardy peasantry attempted to slow down the advance of the Piedmontese army.

Because the *Risorgimento* was predominantly a cultural movement, it was both diverse and flexible. Therefore, the politicians who came to dominate the unification process (for example, Camillo Cavour or Massimo d'Azeglio) could select aspects of the *Risorgimento* that suited their interests and ignore those that did not.

Cavour was not, instinctively, an Italian nationalist. However, he recognised that the conservative political settlement he desired in Italy needed to be wrapped in the loincloth of nationalist sentiment and emotion. In 1860, the Sicilian member of the Chamber of Deputies, Giorgio Asproni, wrote of Cavour that he was 'quite unscrupulous, with no moral restraint [and] incomparable in intrigue'. This is also a fair description of how Cavour treated the ideal of the *Risorgimento* in that he used it to further his own political interests.

THE SIGNIFICANCE OF MAZZINI

Without doubt, Guiseppe Mazzini and the ideal for Italian rebirth that he promoted were of critical importance in providing a model for change and in fostering a national consciousness. However, Mazzini's ideals were revolutionary for their time and his principles stood in direct contrast to those of Cavour, which were conservative. Primarily, Mazzini believed in the creation of a nation state because, through the creation of such states, mankind could be best represented and mankind's interests best served. His was a positive nationalism that stands in stark contrast to the aggressive nationalism of the late-nineteenth and twentieth centuries. To Mazzini, nation states should be based on the principle of democracy, thereby making them fully representative of the people who lived in, and belonged to, those states.

One should understand that Mazzini's views constitute an ideal, and a revolutionary one at that, especially in an Italy and Europe dominated by the conservative Vienna Settlement of 1815. Yet although Mazzini proposed democracy and wished to see the nation state built by 'the people', in reality his views were shared by very few — most of whom belonged to the middle and upper classes. Therefore, even Mazzini's idealism constituted a philosophy imparted from above.

Although the membership of Young Italy set up by Mazzini in 1829 was broader than that of secret societies such as the Carbonari, it was by no means a mass movement. Many of those who took part in the Mazzinian-inspired revolutions of 1821 or 1831, or those such as the Bandera brothers (whose gallant but flawed invasion of Calabria in 1844 led to their martyrdom) were from privileged backgrounds.

It is an irony that the appeal of Mazzinian democracy was so limited. At no time between 1830 and 1871 was the peasantry willing to support a Mazzinian-inspired uprising. This was because the Mazzinian movement had such a narrow social base of support and because it did little by way of proposing a solution to the deep social and economic poverty of many of those living in the Italian states. Indeed, some peasants in Lombardy rose in 1848 against the Austrians and some sections of the Sicilian peasantry took part in the uprisings against King Ferdinand II in 1848. The motivation for the peasantry was land ownership, and therefore economic rather than political. Enclosure of land and the ending of feudal common land rights was a burning issue throughout the 1830s and 1840s in Italy. These had been undertaken by the middle class who were demanding political rights to complement their economic power. There was, therefore, little common ground with the peasantry.

Mazzini made the following speech to workers on 25 July 1848 in Milan. It is very useful in showing the main themes of Mazzinian nationalism, many of which petrified conservative politicians such as Cavour and D'Azeglio. In the first paragraph, Mazzini points out that progress can be achieved only if people come to together. He continues by saying that the most natural group within which people should come together is the nation, and that the future will see the creation of nation states. In the last paragraph Mazzini stresses the importance of patriotism.

Your first duties – first as regards importance – are, as I have already told you, towards Humanity. You are men before you are either citizens or fathers. Embrace the whole human family in your affection. But what can each of you, singly, do for the moral improvement and progress of Humanity? The watchword of the faith of the future is Association, and fraternal co-operation of all towards a common aim; and this is as far superior to all charity, as the edifice which all of you should unite to raise would be superior to the humble hut each one of you might build alone, or with the mere assistance of lending, and borrowing stone, mortar, and tools.

But, you tell me, you cannot attempt united action, distinct and divided as you are in language, customs, tendencies, and capacity. The individual is too insignificant, and Humanity too vast ... This means was provided for you by God when He gave you a country; when, even as a wise overseer of labour distributes the various branches of employment according to the different capacities of the workmen, He divided Humanity into distinct

*groups or nuclei upon the face of the earth, thus creating the germ of
Nationalities. Evil governments have disfigured the divine design.
Nevertheless you may still trace it, distinctly marked out ... They have
disfigured it by their conquests, their greed, and their jealousy even of the
righteous power of others; disfigured it so far that if we except England
and France – there is not perhaps a single country whose present
boundaries correspond to that design.*

*But the Divine design will infallibly be realised. Natural divisions, and
the spontaneous, innate tendencies of the peoples, will take the place of the
arbitrary divisions sanctioned by evil governments. The map of Europe
will be re-drawn. The countries of the Peoples, defined by the vote of free
men, will arise upon the ruins of the countries of kings and privileged
castes, and between these countries harmony and fraternity will exist. And
the common work of Humanity, of general amelioration [improvement]
and the gradual discovery and application of its Law of life, being
distributed according to local development and advance. Then may each
one of you, fortified by the power and the affection of many millions, all
speaking the same language, gifted with the same tendencies, and educated
by the same historical tradition, hope, even by your own single effort, to be
able to benefit all Humanity.*

*O my brothers, love your Country! Our country is our Home, the house
that God has given us, placing therein a numerous family that loves us,
and whom we love; a family with whom we sympathise more readily, and
whom we understand more quickly than we do others; and which, from its
being centred round a given spot, and from the homogeneous nature of its
elements, is adapted to a special branch of activity. Our country is our
common workshop, whence the products of our activity are sent forth for
the benefit of the whole world; wherein the tools and implements of labour
we can most usefully employ are gathered together: nor may we reject
them without disobeying the plan of the Almighty, and diminishing our
own strength.*

THE REVOLUTIONS OF 1848 AND 1849

Despite the social moderation of Mazzinian principles and the limited
scope of their aims, they still posed a real threat to the dominance of
High Politics. The Roman Republic was to be the high point of these
principles and the moment when they were put into reality. Indeed, there
was a world of difference between the clerical rule of Pope Pius IX and
the enlightened but short-lived Roman Republic of 1849.

What Mazzini's government of Rome proved was that his ideals could be
put into practice. In February 1849, the Roman Republic had been

declared and Mazzini hastened to Rome. On arrival, he was given power as part of the triumvirate with Carlo Armellini and Aurelio Saffi. But Mazzini was the driving force of the government. He ordered the clearing of the Roman slums and the redistribution of some Church land. The censorship of the press was abolished, as was the Church's control of education. A constitution was promised. However, it was not issued by the Constituent Assembly until June 1849, by which time it was too late because the republic was on the verge of defeat.

Despite such enlightened government, the Roman Republic had few friends. It was crushed by a French Republic whose president, Louis Napoleon, had taken part in the 1831 uprising in Rome. Now, however, for Louis Napoleon the principles of High Politics dominated and the restoration of the papacy was undertaken in order to please Catholic opinion in France. When the Pope returned to Rome in April 1850, he was welcomed back by cheering crowds. Mazzini's ideas threatened to overturn the social and political order. But there were few people, either in the Italian states or abroad, who wished to see that happen.

The dominance of the institutions of High Politics was challenged in 1848–9. However, it is clear that the challenge varied in its aims. For example, in Piedmont the challenge focused around the removal of the Austrians. In Sicily, the demands revolved around the resurrection of the 1812 constitution. Although seemingly threatening, the revolutionaries were, in reality, limited in their political and social ambitions.

However, we have to be careful not to impose the values of the twenty-first century on to those of the mid-nineteenth century. On the surface, the actions of the Roman Republic in 1849 were relatively moderate. The Church's power was attacked in February 1849 with the abolition of its temporal power and the announcement of Rome as a secular state. But to many across Europe, the deposition of Pius IX was a revolutionary action that disturbed the *status quo*. For this reason, the French National Assembly, which had been elected by universal suffrage, voted to send a force in 1849 to restore the Pope.

There is little evidence of a desire among the revolutionaries of 1848 to establish a united Italy. In that sense it was not a politically motivated series of revolutions. There were clearly economic grievances: the disappointing harvests of 1845 and 1846 had left grain prices high and created the context of discontent. The reformism of Pius IX in 1846–7 was a means to the end of strengthening papal rule of the Papal States. It also acted as a trigger to demands for reform in other areas of Italy, most noticeably Tuscany and Piedmont.

What is most striking is the conservatism of the first wave of revolutions of 1848, not just in Italy but across Europe. In Sicily and Naples, the uprisings and granting of liberal constitutions did not represent a social revolution. In Vienna, the March revolution and the overthrow of Metternich were to have an important political impact, but the propertied classes remained in control across the Habsburg Empire. In Milan, in March 1848, some of the fiercest street fighting took place. But the Milanese provisional government led by Carlo Cattaneo had no desire to call for a republic. Instead, it turned to the Piedmontese monarchy and Charles Albert for protection. This is as good an example as any other event of the limitations of the revolutionary aspirations of 1848. Even though the leader of the uprising in Venice, Daniel Manin, was a 'democrat', the revolution he declared proceeded cautiously and in July 1848 also rallied under the banner of Charles Albert. In the end, Manin acted to restrain as much as provoke.

In *The Risorgimento* (1962) by **Agatha Ramm**, the author concludes that 'the rebels of 1848–9 were not the kind of men to aim at a revolutionary shift of social power'. She is nearly, but not entirely, correct. Most of the revolutionaries who came to dominate the revolutions of 1848–9 had the limited objective of constitutional reform. Yet even Mazzini recognised there was little appetite among the masses for democratic republicanism. Even Garibaldi's army of volunteers, which performed so heroically against the French in defence of Rome in the summer of 1849, contained few labourers or peasants. Indeed, what is striking is the consistency of apathy among the common people of Rome for political change from 1848 to 1871. Those democrats such as Professor Montanelli, who argued in 1849 for a single constitutionally united Italy, managed to achieve the aim of the creation of a *Costituente*, but precious little else. Although the new assembly received delegates from across the Papal States and Tuscany, it found little support elsewhere.

Mazzini was to create an ideal that threatened those in power. Therefore, over the coming years elements of his message were adopted, distorted, manipulated and misused by the agents of High Politics, most noticeably Cavour. In *Italy: A Modern History* (1959), **Denis Mack-Smith** clearly argues how the pragmatism of Cavour was eventually able to translate 'Mazzini's dogma into practical politics'. The achievement of the Roman Republic was that it created a legend of heroic but worthwhile failure in the direct action against perceived oppression. But 1848–9 also highlighted the weakness of Mazzinian tactics, the limited support for revolution and the unlikelihood of a 'people's war' to liberate Italy.

Those who were serious in support of political change in Italy began to look to Piedmont with its liberal constitution and increasingly modern economy. It was also Piedmont that would be most likely to enrol the foreign support necessary to remove Austria. After 1848, many 'democrats' such as Giorgio Pallavicino came to a pragmatic conclusion about the future of the Italian nation. In the following extract, from a letter dated 18 November 1851, Pallavicino is writing to General Pepe, who led the military forces of the Pope in 1848. It is a most instructive passage.

> I, like you, believe that the life of a people lies in independence more than in liberty. But as an Italian first and foremost, I seek Italian forces for an Italian war, and a popular insurrection would not be enough for the purpose. We have seen this already: a popular rising can win temporary victories within the confines of its own cities, but without a miracle it cannot fight and defeat regular troops in the open countryside.

> To defeat cannons and soldiers you need cannons and soldiers of your own. You needs arms, not Mazzinian chatter.

> Piedmont has got soldiers and cannons; therefore I am Piedmontese. Piedmont, by ancient custom, tradition, character and duty, is today a monarchy; therefore I am not a republican. And I am content with Charles Albert's constitution.

(Extract taken from G. Pallavicino, *Memorie* (Turin, 1886))

CONCLUSION

The German Karl Marx wrote that the Roman Republic had been 'an attempt against property, against the bourgeois order'. That 'bourgeois order', both in Italy and elsewhere, stood resolute against the development of Mazzinian principles and the emergence of a democratic Italy. For Charles Albert of Piedmont and his successor Victor Emmanuel II, the lessons of 1848 were that foreign dominance of Italy could only be ended with outside support. Such support would only be forthcoming if Mazzinianism was kept in check. As we will see in Section 2, the challenge for Cavour was not so much how to unify Italy but how to isolate those on the political extremes of Italian politics that might threaten the established order and upset his carefully laid diplomatic plans. The process of the unification of Italy from 1848 to 1871 was, in part, as much to do with the defeat of Mazzinianism as it was the creation of an Italian nation state.

SECTION 2

What were the roles played by Cavour and Garibaldi in the unification of Italy?

KEY POINTS

- Cavour was one of the central characters of the unification process. His contribution to the economic modernisation of Piedmont was especially significant.
- As a diplomat, Cavour was often forced to respond to events as much as provoke change. However, his consummate skill, especially in the critical years 1859 and 1860, were of fundamental importance in shaping the Italian nation.
- However, Cavour should not be considered an Italian nationalist. He was primarily a political pragmatist.
- Garibaldi's significance was to turn the unification of the northern regions of Italy into unification of the whole peninsula. It was also to act as a thorn in the side of the more cautious conservatives.

MACK-SMITH ON CAVOUR

In the biography *Cavour* (1985), **Denis Mack-Smith** paints a portrait of Cavour as an architect of the unification of Italy. According to Mack-Smith, Cavour was the arch diplomat and a brilliant political operator. He also identified Cavour's great strength as the ability to manage Parliament. Indeed, the forging of the *connubio* was Cavour's master trick. It gave him the legitimacy of Parliamentary support for his actions and from that support he derived his considerable authority.

In one of the most enlightening sections of his book, Mack-Smith identified that Cavour was a bundle of contradictions. On the one hand he was a conservative, but on the other he occasionally resorted to revolutionary action. He could also be idealistic and cynical, kind but ruthless, cautious and occasionally audacious.

Part of the proof of Cavour's limited nationalist ambitions was the nature of the constitution imposed on Italy in 1861. In *Cavour* (1985), Mack-Smith is generous in his interpretation that the constitutional settlement was created by the speed with which unification took place between 1859 and 1861. Indeed, Mack-Smith goes so far as to stress that, at heart, Cavour was a believer in 'decentralisation' of power but for pragmatic reasons acted otherwise. Mack-Smith also pointed to Cavour's decision in 1860 to ask Ministers of the Interior Farini and Minghetti to conduct an investigation into the possibility of some kind of regional autonomy. Their proposals included a plan for some form of devolution with regional governors and assemblies. At a local level mayors would be elected. However, the scheme was half-hearted and eventually dismissed in 1861 by the new Italian Parliament. That said, Mack-Smith does recognise that despite promising some degree of autonomy to Tuscany and Sicily for much of 1860, in the end Cavour 'never went out of his way to push it politically'.

CAVOUR AND PIEDMONTISATION

In Cavour's defence, one can argue that the decision to impose Piedmontisation was taken when he was out of office in late 1859. The government of Alfonso La Marmora had to decide quickly how Lombardy would be governed. It decided to impose the Piedmontese administrative model on Lombardy without any debate and by emergency degree. In Modena, in August 1860, a popular assembly controlled by Farini voted for annexation to Piedmont. However, there is little evidence to suggest that Cavour disapproved of these developments. He did nothing to reverse them when he came into power, despite the fact that such centralisation caused considerable disquiet.

In *The Italian Risorgimento* (1998), **Martin Clark** suggests there was so little sympathy from Cavour and politicians of his type for regional government or a federal state because of the dominant localist mentality. Clark argues that Italian politicians were concerned about their own municipalities rather than their 'regions', let alone regions elsewhere. He goes on to point out that Cavour only went to Tuscany once and never further south. Yet to suggest that Cavour's decisions should be put down to a narrow localist mentality does not sit comfortably with the fact that he was well informed and understood issues relevant to the world outside Piedmont. He also shared the view of many in the Piedmontese Parliament that local autonomy equalled national collapse.

Cavour did not always dismiss the idea of a federal Italian state. However, the ultimate motivating force in his acceptance of such a proposal was political pragmatism. At Plombières, in July 1858, Cavour struck a deal with Louis Napoleon that linked the promise of French support to expel Austria from northern Italy with the handing over to France of Savoy and, as agreed after the meeting, Nice. It was also agreed at Plombières that Italy would become a federation of states: the Kingdom of Upper

Italy which was Piedmont writ large; the Kingdom of Central Italy; the Kingdom of Naples; and a reduced Papal States. The leader of this federation would be the Pope, mainly as compensation for the loss of land to the Kingdom of Central Italy. It is often assumed that this model of Italian political development was devised by Louis Napoleon. However, this has been disputed by some historians. In *Italy in the Age of the Risorgimento 1790–1870* (1983), **Harry Hearder** asserts that 'the creative mind behind the decisions reached at Plombières was Cavour's rather than Napoleon'. His evidence is the memoranda that Cavour took with him to Plombières which accurately predicts the course and outcome of the meeting.

LOUIS NAPOLEON

There is little doubt that Louis Napoleon was keen to help Piedmont in its struggle with Austria. It is correct to assume that the blueprint of a federal Italy was attractive to the French Emperor, because it made likely the possibility of a French rather than Austrian-dominated peninsula. The preservation of some of the papacy's temporal power and the offer of the presidency of the Italian federation to the Pope would, hopefully for Louis Napoleon, keep Catholic opinion in France relatively content. There is also little doubt that Louis Napoleon looked for territorial gain, and Savoy was the perfect prize. All of this was anticipated by Cavour, who was not too concerned with the loss of Savoy, given that the majority of the population spoke a French dialect. It is likely that the most important aspect of the treaty for Louis Napoleon was the furthering of his dynastic ambitions with the arrangement of the marriage of his nephew Prince Jerome to Princess Clotilde.

Given Cavour's satisfaction with the Plombières agreement and given his determination to see it implemented, one might assume that the political settlement it proposed was close to his own views. In that case, it is clear that Cavour was not an Italian nationalist in the sense that he agreed with the idea of the political unification of the whole peninsula. The limits of his nationalism were confined to the wish to expel the Austrians from Lombardy and Venetia, and to unite the freed provinces into a potentially wealthy political entity.

At Plombières, Cavour was reluctant to discuss the French annexation of Nice because he was aware that the reaction of those nationally minded to the loss of an Italian dialect-speaking province would be considerable, especially to Garibaldi who was born in Nice. However, at the Treaty of Turin in March 1860, Cavour was content to sign over Savoy and Nice to France in return for Lombardy. This was despite the fact that he was not obliged to do so by the terms of the Plombières agreement, as Louis

Napoleon had failed to keep his side of the bargain and push the Austrians out of Venice. However, his diplomatic instincts were sufficient to tell him that the key to Piedmontese strength was the continual support, however erratic, of Louis Napoleon.

As already stated, Cavour was a pragmatist. He was also politically astute. His defining and most significant attribute was his ability to respond to events and to understand the opportunities that these events presented to Piedmont. The clearest case in point was the issue of the annexation of the central Italian duchies by Piedmont in 1860. Such an annexation was not foreseen by Cavour or Louis Napoleon at Plombières. Neither was the annexation particularly acceptable to the French, given the fact it changed the balance of power foreseen by Plombières and, thereby, reduced the possibility of French influence. Hence the Treaty of Turin and the surrendering of Nice to France.

In Tuscany, Baron Ricasoli had ensured that there was little chance of Leopold II returning to reclaim his duchy and, in August 1860, the Tuscan assembly (which was heavily under Ricasoli's influence) asked to be annexed to Piedmont. In Modena, the leadership of Farini ensured the same request in the same month.

CAVOUR AND POPULAR CONSENT

In order to legitimise the annexation of central Italy, Cavour came up with the idea that it should take place through popular consent. Such an idea was, of course, a direct contradiction of his real beliefs. The idea of self-determination, that the peoples of Italy would determine their own future, smacked of Mazzinianism. However, Cavour was wise enough to realise that he could borrow the language of popular change and some of its trappings (for example, plebiscites) for his own ends. Cavour understood that the idea of holding plebiscites would be acceptable to the British government led by Lord Palmerston and Bonapartist France, and he was right. He also understood that the votes could be fixed through intimidation, corruption and bullying. The fact that there was an organisation, the National Society, willing to do Cavour's dirty work made it much easier for him to distance himself from some pretty strange results.

In April 1860, the vote in Italian-speaking Nice against annexation resulted in only 160 votes against. For Cavour, the important issue was not that the Piedmontese-dominated Italian state was larger than originally intended. The work of Ricasoli and Farini had ensured that the political settlement in Tuscany and Emilia, both strategically important states, was to be a conservative one. Cavour recognised the political vacuum that existed and he had the incentive of securing a conservative settlement for the longer term through annexation. By doing so he could prevent the possibility of a more democratic settlement on Mazzinian lines. It is no wonder that Mazzini dismissed Cavour's plans as a 'paltry, hateful programme of expediency'. But Cavour was simply doing what he did best: fulfilling the art of the possible.

CAVOUR AND GARIBALDI

Perhaps the most contentious examples of Cavour's pragmatism was his reaction to Garibaldi's invasion of Sicily and Naples in 1860. In *The Risorgimento* (1962), the historian **Agatha Ramm** argued that 'it was due to Cavour that any of the aims of the *Risorgimento* were achieved, but it was due to him, some of the richness of the *Risorgimento* was inevitably lost'. This is not surprising, as Cavour stood against so much of what Garibaldi believed in and rejected the 'democratic' element of the *Risorgimento* that Garibaldi so fervently supported. It is clear that throughout the episode, Cavour struggled to regain control of the situation. In *Cavour* (1985), **Denis Mack-Smith** suggests that Cavour's inaction in preventing Garibaldi sailing from Genoa on 6 May 1860 was part of a wider political paralysis, leaving Cavour in a dangerous predicament. If he was seen to help Garibaldi he would run the risk of alienating France and moderate opinion in Piedmont, which feared the consequences of Garibaldi's revolutionary activity. If he refused to support such a popular adventure he would be seen to be restraining action undertaken in the Italian interest. In a letter dated 16 May 1860, and addressed to fellow politician Ricasoli, Cavour clearly expressed the difficulty of his situation.

> [Garibaldi] *cannot be stopped from making war on the Kingdom of Naples. It may be good, it may be bad, but it was inevitable. If we had tried to restrain Garibaldi by force he would have become a real domestic problem. Now what will happen? It is impossible to predict. Will England help him? It is possible. Will France oppose him? I don't think so. And what about us? We cannot support him openly, nor can we encourage private efforts on his behalf ... I fully recognise all of the disadvantages of the ambiguous line that we are adopting, but I cannot work out any other policy that doesn't have even greater dangers.*

Cavour's letter reveals only half the truth to Ricasoli. He did work out another policy, that of interference through agents. His policy of interference became more effective once he recognised and accepted the idea of a united Italy, north and south.

Prompted by Louis Napoleon, Cavour worked behind the scenes for an alliance with the Bourbons against Garibaldi. In June 1860, he sent messages to King Francesco of Naples suggesting an alliance. At the same time, though, his agents were working hard in Naples attempting to provoke an uprising against the Bourbons that would justify Piedmontese intervention. Simultaneously, Cavour was working hard to contain the impact of Garibaldi's actions. Although he was prepared to entertain the possibility of a united peninsula, he was not prepared to accept it as a democratic Italy. Garibaldi launched his invasion of the Italian mainland in August 1860 in the name of 'Victor Emmanuel and Italy'. However, it was not the Italy envisaged by a far more conservative Cavour.

Once it was clear that Garibaldi's invasion of Sicily was a success, Cavour attempted to influence events through agents. His first emissary to Sicily was La Farina, a leader of the National Society and a Sicilian. This was not a good choice, given that La Farina had supported the transfer of Nice to France. On 7 July 1860, La Farina was expelled from Sicily by Cavour and was replaced by future prime minister, Agostino Depretis.

It was Cavour's ability to gamble when necessary that secured the Italy of his liking. As Garibaldi's invasion of the mainland proved to be a success, so the urgency of the situation for Cavour became even greater. It was important for Cavour that he was seen to support Garibaldi. The king and many in the Piedmontese Parliament hailed Garibaldi's actions in

Portrait of Count Camillo de Cavour by M. Gordigiani.

Giuseppe Garibaldi at Caprera in 1865.

liberating the south from the rule of the despotic Bourbons. On 9 August 1860, Cavour wrote:

> *Garibaldi has rendered Italy the greatest services that a man could give her: he has given Italians confidence in themselves. He has proved to Europe that Italians know how to fight and die on the battlefield to reconquer a fatherland.*

One factor hindering Cavour's attempts to stall Garibaldi's triumphant march north was the relative unpopularity among Neapolitans of the idea of annexation by Piedmont. In July 1860, Cavour sent agents to Naples with orders to provoke an uprising that would be the pretext for a Piedmontese take-over. It was not forthcoming, the population of Naples preferring to wait for liberation by Garibaldi.

However, Cavour knew that Garibaldi's ultimate target was Rome, not Naples. He understood that the events of 1849 had left an indelible mark on the great adventurer's mind and that the appeal of the rallying cry '*Roma o morte*' was as great in 1860 as it had been eleven years earlier. Yet an invasion of the Papal States by a democratic-inspired force would destroy Cavour's diplomatic initiative. The threat of such an invasion was real. Not only did Garibaldi possess a force some 20,000 strong (and possibly greater), but also a force some 9000 strong led by Agostino Bertani (a supporter of Mazzini) had amassed on the border of the Papal States. Cavour's clear option was to invade the Papal States in order to forestall any further action on Garibaldi's behalf. Even if this meant upsetting the Pope and possibly the French, it was a risk Cavour felt he should take.

In 1948, the historian **Gaetano Salvemini** wrote in *Mazzini* (1948) that the unification of Italy was not the result of a harmony of ideas born of the *Risorgimento* but of a struggle: 'In reality there was in the struggle a winner and a loser; the winner was Cavour, the loser Mazzini.'

Salvemini was suggesting that the victory was that of the moderates rather than the democrats. However, he was under no illusions how this happened, claiming that Italy was unified 'by the knife of Shylock'. The invasion of the Papal States by Piedmontese forces in September 1860 was Cavour's masterstroke. On his orders, an uprising in the Papal States was engineered and the Piedmontese invited in. From that moment the creation of an Italy based on Cavour's vision rather than Garibaldi's or Mazzini's was assured.

Despite Garibaldi's astonishing success in defeating the Bourbon army at the Battle of Volturno on 26 October 1860, it was the Piedmontese victory at Castelfidaro a month earlier that decided the fate of the south.

The speed with which Cavour had plebiscites organised and the extent to which they were, again, fixed is evidence of his political effectiveness. In reality, Garibaldi was outmanoeuvred.

In *Italy: A Modern History* (1959), **Denis Mack-Smith** points out how a deputy of the Italian Parliament referred to Cavour as 'a cross between **Robert Peel and Machiavelli**'. He stressed, quite correctly, that Cavour's actions in 1860 were not of a man with a desire to see Italy unified. Indeed, he acted because, as Mack-Smith pointed out, 'he disliked revolutionary republicanism more than he loved national unity'. As a result, he responded to Garibaldi's invasion of the mainland with a strategy aimed at 'outdoing [the revolutionaries] at their own game'.

CAVOUR'S EPITAPH

Cavour's political skill was attacked once he had died. He was considered by many to be scheming and manipulative. In *Cavour* (1985), **Denis Mack-Smith** points to the fact that the British politician and (later) prime minister **Benjamin Disraeli** called Cavour 'utterly unscrupulous'. While this is somewhat rich coming from Disraeli, the view from Palmerston on the other side of the British House of Commons was far warmer. He stated that Cavour was 'one of the most distinguished patriots [to] have adorned the history of any country'. However, both fell into the trap of judging Cavour by what happened during the process of unification.

Cavour was not the 'patriot' Palmerston believed him to be. His ambitions were far more narrow. Indeed Mack-Smith, falls into the same trap at the end of his excellent biography by stressing Cavour's 'ability to manage Parliament … [skill] in foreign policy and … sheer virtuosity in every branch of the political arts'. This list is undoubtedly accurate. However, added to it should be Cavour's foresight in developing the infrastructure of Piedmont and especially the communication system. Cavour was a consummate politician, but he was also the foremost and first moderniser. The reduction of tariffs and the switch to a greater degree of free trade created better relations with countries such as Britain and France, with whom trade treaties had been signed by the end of 1851.

Equally significant as free trade was the confidence in the Piedmontese economy caused by Cavour's intelligence and foresight. The most important aspect of his policy was the construction of the railways. The impact of building the railways on the economies of Europe should not be underestimated. Similarly, the extent of railway building was a good indicator of the extent of economic modernisation in any one state in the nineteenth century. In the year of Italian unification there were still only

2404 kilometres of railway line in Italy, which was the equivalent of 0.096 kilometre per inhabitant (in Britain the figure was 0.74). Around 40 per cent of the lines were in Piedmont, giving it a clear claim to economic leadership.

It was always Cavour's belief that economic leadership, and railway construction especially, were a prerequisite of political power. In an article written in 1846, he expressed the view that the inevitable railway network that would soon be built on the Italian peninsula would lead to the development of a greater awareness of Italian nationality. The challenge he laid down to Charles Albert was to be the leader in that process.

When he became prime minister, Cavour threw the weight of political support behind a programme of railway construction. He also encouraged the investment of foreign capital into Piedmont, the majority of it being French. Indeed, the line between Turin and Genoa that was opened in 1854 was funded by French capital, in particular money invested by the bankers Rothschild. Similarly, the Mont Cenis tunnel, started in 1857, was financed by a number of Parisian-based bankers including Laffitte and Rothschild. The importance of such an arrangement should not be underestimated. Influential French finance had an important stake in the financial and economic well-being and expansion of the Piedmontese railways and Piedmont.

CONCLUSION

The impact of Cavour on the process of Italian unity should not be underestimated. He was the consummate Parliamentary politician and a politician of his time. In the mid-nineteenth century, few leading political figures were prepared to accept or even foresee the advent of mass politics. Cavour's legacy was to create a political structure and culture that would suit Italy's needs for the next half century and that would only be fully undermined with the advent of mass political parties. His role as a diplomat is much highlighted and has been written about extensively. Yet it could be argued that his greatest contribution to the *Risorgimento* was not as architect of Italian unity but as moderniser of Piedmont. In helping to create a modern political state with an semi-industrial economy he helped to lay the foundations of the unification process.

SECTION 3

What led to the failure of the Church, 1848–71?

KEY POINTS

- In 1871, Pope Pius IX announced to a despairing Catholic world that he was 'a prisoner in the Vatican'. He also left his audience in no doubt that the Church's anger was directed at the new state of Italy.
- However, the anti-clericalism of the state was only partly to blame for this state of clerical isolation. By its own actions, and especially those of Pius IX, the Church had done much to hasten the loss of its temporal power.
- But one must be careful not to exaggerate the extent of the demise of the Church as a force to be reckoned with in Italy. As the Church's temporal power slipped, its hold on the spiritual lives of Italians strengthened.

1871

In *The Italian Risorgimento* (1998), **Martin Clark** argues that the Catholic Church was 'among the big losers of the *Risorgimento*'. However, one should be careful not to argue that the failure of the Church in Italy was by any means total. On the surface, Clark's view is correct, most obviously in 1871 when the armies of the Italian state invaded Rome and the papacy lost its temporal power. The loss of temporal power was an important issue because, to the Church, the Pope could not be governed by anyone else on earth.

The humiliation of the Church was apparent in 1871 when Rome was seized. In May 1871, the state issued the Law of Guarantees, which was an attempt to define the relations between Church and state. The pope was given some sovereignty in that he was granted the status of a monarch; was allowed his own postal services; had full liberty for his religious functions; his representatives at the Vatican were given full diplomatic status and would be given 3,225,000 lire a year compensation for the loss of temporal lands. However, Pius IX chose to ignore the deal because the proposals were made by a state that had control of Rome and had seized the Papal States.

GIOBERTI

The creation of an Italian state under the leadership of the Piedmontese monarchy was not inevitable. Indeed, for much of the middle part of the nineteenth century, the Pope was assumed to be the natural leader of any Italian state. Highly influential in the development of this line of thought was Vincenzo Gioberti. The publication in 1843 of *Primato Morale e Civile degli Italiani* was to have widespread consequences. In the book, Gioberti argued in favour of Italian independence – the creation of an Italian federation under the leadership of the Pope. His ideas were a strong influence on Count Cesare Balbo, whose book *Hopes of Italy* (1844) took Gioberti's logic one step further by suggesting that this could be achieved through diplomacy.

The significance of both books is that they argued that liberation of the Italian peoples could and should come from above and should result in a far more conservative settlement than suggested by Mazzini. Therefore, they represent a very significant development in the *Risorgimento*. No longer should it be dominated by the tactic of popular uprising. The debate was now open to the possibility of political change engineered from above. Such a blueprint was to attract the interest of Pius IX, at least for a while, and later Cavour.

It was not just Gioberti who asserted the primacy of the Pope. Further evidence can be seen at Plombières in 1859, when Napoleon insisted that the Italian federation he envisaged would be led by Pius IX. This was not just Napoleon pleasing the Catholics in France. The papacy's spiritual position as the leader of the world's foremost faith, and the importance of Catholic opinion in France, Austria and parts of Germany, made the Pope seem the natural leader. One should also remember that the Pope ruled over a considerable part of central Italy as a feudal lord.

However, it was not so much Piedmontese anti-clericalism that led to the decline of the papacy's temporal power, but the actions of the papacy itself. A crucial turning point was the issuing of the Allocution in April 1848. In reality, the Allocution was a statement of neutrality. Pius IX was particularly concerned that his army, led by General Durando, had marched out of the Papal States on 25 April to join the Piedmontese army in its fight against Austria. But if the aim of the Allocution was simply a reaction to this event, then its impact went far deeper. Indeed, one might argue that Pius was reacting to Durando's decision to fight the Austrians and that he was attempting to send signals to Vienna disowning the actions of his own general. However, disclaiming war against Austria severely undermined the papacy's claim to lead the Italian cause.

THE IMPACT OF THE ALLOCUTION

The Allocution was a turning point on the road to a united Italy because it revealed the weaknesses of the papacy's position regarding temporal power. But this was not simply an issue in 1848. In *Modern Italy 1871–1995* (1996), the historian **Martin Clark** points out that the papacy's loosening grip on temporal power was inevitable. The aftermath of the 1831 revolution was of importance in the decline of papal temporal power. The fact that Austrian troops remained in Bologna until 1838 was less traumatic than the systematic pillage of the Marshes and Romagna by papal troops. Indeed, such was the extent of atrocity that the historian **Harry Hearder** commented in *Italy in the Age of the Risorgimento 1790–1870* (1983), that the actions of the papal troops 'thereby prepared the way not only for the revolutions of 1848, but also for the ultimate extinction of the [Pope's] temporal power'.

The critical point behind the Allocution of 1848 was that it marked the end of any dream held by moderates and those who ascribed to the ideas of Gioberti that the Pope might lead the nationalist cause in Italy. It also severely weakened the idea of the Pope as head of an Italian federation, for integral to that role was an element of antagonism towards Austria. However, nationalist expectations of Pius IX were inflated. Similarly, it was inaccurate to portray Pius as a 'liberal' Pope. He had been influenced by the ideas of Gioberti's *Primato* (1843) and shared in the belief in the primacy of the papacy in temporal affairs. His reforms – including the freeing of political prisoners in 1846, the appointment of Cardinal Gizzi as secretary in the same year, the creation of the customs union and the reduction in press censorship 1847 – were examples of measures that, on the surface, seemed to point in the direction of a more liberal papacy.

However, one has to question Pius IX's intentions. His predecessor, Gregory XVI, and Gregory's secretary, Cardinal Lambruschini, had crushed all aspirations for civil liberty. Pius IX should be seen as liberal and advanced compared to the rule of the Papal States by his predecessors. But the impulse for Pius IX's reforms was not to liberalise the papacy, because attempting to do so would only weaken its authority. Reform was undertaken to strengthen the papacy's popularity and its temporal and spiritual power.

THE SYLLABUS OF ERRORS

On closer inspection, the problem was not Pius IX's lack of liberalism. It was that liberal, nationalist and some historians' expectations of Pius IX were, and are, too great. Instead of focusing on the 1846–8 period, in which Pius IX worked to establish himself politically, it is far more informative to look at his actions in the 1860s and 1870s. Perhaps the most instructive document issued during the papacy of Pius IX was the *Syllabus of Errors* of 1864.

The *Syllabus* was a direct criticism of the main tenets of liberalism. It attacked religious toleration, freedom of expression and thought, as well as all the 'isms' of the nineteenth century – including socialism, liberalism, nationalism and communism. At the heart of the *Syllabus* was the assertion that neither the papacy nor Catholics as a whole should accept 'progress, liberalism, and modern civilisation'. It might be argued that the *Syllabus* was the result of the increased threat to the Church's temporal power as signalled by the creation of the state of Italy in 1861. However, it is clear that Pius IX's interests were always primarily spiritual and that he had a particular preoccupation with Mary, mother of Jesus Christ.

The most significant appointment Pius IX made during his reign as Pope was that of Cardinal Antonelli as his Secretary of State in 1848. Antonelli's conservatism matched that of his master and it is incorrect to assume that one was more conservative than the other. Indeed, the severity of Pius IX's rule has seemingly been overlooked. For example, **public execution** in the Papal States by beheading was commonplace.

KEY EVENT

Public execution
In 1855, a man called De Felici attempted to kill Antonelli. He failed in his attempt, but was executed none the less.

The real significance of Antonelli was to persuade Pius to resist attacks on the Church's temporal power. In *Ad apostolicae*, Pius argued that temporal power was justified by the teachings of Christ and was therefore non-negotiable. However, neither Pius nor Antonelli were rigid in their adherence to this viewpoint. In 1861, negotiations between Church and state about the future of Rome took place, but were broken off due to a healthy mistrust between the two.

Given its lack of military power and deep conservatism in an age of liberalism and nationalism, it is not surprising that the Church failed to hold on to its temporal power. However, the uneasy relationship between Church and state, aptly termed 'fractious cohabitation' by **Martin Clark** in *Modern Italy 1871–1995* (1996), did less damage to the Church than the state. Indeed, it acted to strengthen the Church's grip over spiritual affairs. The response of the Church authorities to the increasing state anti-clericalism in Piedmont was to suggest that Catholics abstain from participating in politics. In 1858, a Catholic newspaper editor, Don Margotti, argued that Catholics should be 'neither electors nor elected'. Papal independence was asserted by Pius IX's rejection of the Law of Guarantees in 1871, despite the fact that the offer made to the papacy included a guarantee of monarchical status, a substantial income and independence of action.

By rejecting such a compromise and adopting the image of the 'prisoner in the Vatican', Pius cleverly asserted the distinctiveness of the Church. In 1874, he even threatened to excommunicate any Catholic who voted in state elections. This paved the way for the emergence of a distinct Catholic culture including institutions such as schools and hospitals and powerful lay groups such as *Opera dei Congressi*. The dominance of the culture by a papacy strengthened by papal infallibility was to give it power and influence that lasted well into the twentieth century.

THREATS TO THE PAPACY

The response of Pius IX and his advisers to the emergence of the nation state was, on the one hand, deeply reactionary and, on the other, astute. Pius IX' s attempts to halt the advance of nationalism and the other 'isms' of the nineteenth century so roundly condemned in the *Syllabus of Errors* are reminiscent of King Canute's forlorn attempts to turn back the waves. Yet while doing so and, meanwhile, strengthening and reinforcing its spiritual leadership, Pius laid the foundations for the future strength of the Catholic Church in Italy and beyond.

Without doubt, throughout the trials and tribulations of the *Risorgimento* the overriding aim of Pius IX was to protect the power of the papacy. One of Pius and Cardinal Antonelli's greatest concerns was that a number of Catholics across Europe were liberals. After the defeat of Austria in 1866 by Prussia, German Catholics were vulnerable to criticism by a protestant Prussian government that might question their loyalty to the new north German state. However, Pius' concern was that, in an age of the developing nation state, Catholics would be forced to choose between the nation state and the papacy or would have split loyalty. Hence the introduction of papal infallibility in 1870 as the ultimate attempt of the papacy to shore up its influence over Catholics across Europe.

The Church was not just under threat from the increasing power of the state. The loss of temporal power as a result of the political unification of Italy was a bitter blow. Its spiritual supremacy was also under attack from the advance of scientific thought and theory. Therefore, the *Syllabus of Errors* of 1864, papal infallibility of 1870 and the increasingly defensive attitude of Pius IX's papacy should be seen as desperate attempts to protect the dominance of the Church in spiritual matters from the increasingly aggressive advance of science. The belief put forward by Charles Darwin in *The Origin of Species* (1859) that humankind evolved was a direct challenge to the theory of Creation as explained in *Genesis* in the Bible. Similarly challenging was the view held by those such as French Catholic Ernest Renan in the early 1860s that the Bible should not be treated as a completely accurate history of events. Indeed, part of the

Syllabus of Errors was centred on a defence of orthodox Catholic views against Darwinism. The Church felt under considerable threat, which is reflected in its calling of the Vatican Council of 1869 – the first such event since the Council of Trent called in 1545 in the face of the threat from the Protestant reformation.

Yet it is possible to argue that the double onslaught of science and the birth of the nation state revitalised the Church. The loss of land to the state after 1861 and the closing of many religious monasteries and convents inspired the surviving Church to act. By 1900 there were 12,000 more nuns in Italy than there had been in 1870. Additionally, the *Opera dei Congressi* had a considerable influence on Italian society through the running of schools to rural banks.

CONCLUSION

When the state attacked the Church's role in Italian society, the Church fought back. A clear example came in 1890, when the Italian prime minister, Francesco Crispi, introduced a major reform of charities as a means of excluding Church organisations from undertaking some of their traditional functions. The response of Pope Leo XIII was to issue the encyclical *Rerum Novarum* in 1891, which encouraged Catholics to become involved in social reform and improvement in order to stem the rise of socialism and combat the worst side effects of capitalism. It is clear that the loss of temporal power paved the way for the Church to become involved in spheres of influence that were to its liking.

SECTION 4

What was the role and impact of foreign powers?

KEY POINTS

- The impact of foreign powers on the political shape and destiny of Italy was considerable. From the Vienna Settlement 1815 until the mid- to late 1850s, Austrian dominance of the peninsula was the strongest barrier to political change.
- The disintegration of the Vienna Settlement played an important part in hastening political change in Italy. The Crimean War was an important watershed. Thereafter, France and Britain had a greater influence over the course of political change in Italy.
- The change in the balance of power in Europe and especially the rise of Prussia acted in the interests of those who wished to unify Italy.

The importance of diplomacy in forging the shape of the new Italian state is clear. In *The Struggle for Mastery in Europe 1848–1918* (1954), **A.J.P. Taylor** stresses that Cavour's greatest achievement was to recognise that: 'The Italian Question was a problem in international relations, not in domestic politics … Italy could not make herself; she could only be made by exploiting the differences between the Great Power.' While this is an astute judgement, it does not necessarily mean that Italy was unified by diplomatic design. Instead, it is more appropriate to argue that the series of events, the change in the balance of European powers and the sympathetic attitude of many of the most significant policy makers at the time would, together, act in favour of those who wished to see the creation of an Italian state.

However, it is too simplistic to suggest that foreign powers intervened in Italian affairs actively to promote the cause of Italian unity, because they did not. Rather, they intervened in order to promote their own interests. Italy was, and is, strategically importantly placed. The influence and significance of the papacy on domestic affairs in many parts of Europe should not be underestimated.

THE ROLE OF FRANCE

The role of France is often highlighted as being of central importance to the cause of Italian unity. The romantic attachment supposedly held by

Louis Napoleon to the cause of Italian unity is often suggested as a critical factor in explaining how unification came about in 1861. Indeed, the evidence in favour of this line of argument is strong.

In 1831, Louis Napoleon had hatched a plan to overthrow the rulers of Italy and declare his cousin Napoleon (who was Napoleon I's only legitimate son) 'King of Italy'. The only snag was that, at the time, his cousin was a prisoner of Austria, which meant that Louis Napoleon would have to rule as regent. In 1859, Louis Napoleon had redrafted a speech written by Cavour, which was to be read by Victor Emmanuel in the wake of Plombières. The last sentence, written by Louis Napoleon, read: 'We cannot remain insensitive to the cries of pain which comes to us from so many parts of Italy.'

Similarly, the Plombières agreement itself, in which Louis Napoleon committed France to the cause of expelling the Austrians, can be seen as a crucial turning point. However, the issue is one of intention. In *The Risorgimento* (1959), **Agatha Ramm** argues that 'Napoleon was almost equally as much a liability as an asset' to the cause of Italian unity. His desire to go to war against Austria in 1859 was not to relieve the 'cries of pain' but, as Ramm argued, 'to draw diplomatic profit from the war'. By 1859, the settlement imposed on Europe by the Treaty of Vienna was dated and crumbling. By embarking on his adventurous policy in Italy, Napoleon was recognising that Austrian power could be challenged without sparking a revolution. However, Plombières and even the events of 1831 reveal that French involvement in Italy was in part undertaken for dynastic reasons. The marriage of Prince Jerome to Clotilde was as important as any other clause to Napoleon at Plombières. He was prepared to allow for a deferment on the issue of the transferral of Nice to France, but not on the idea of securing the dynastic future of the Bonaparte family. This was a preoccupation of his uncle Napoleon I and reflected the family insecurity.

More important for Napoleon than the ideal of Italian national unity was the popularity he felt he could gain at home through a successful foreign policy in Italy. Elections in France in May 1857 showed his imperial regime to be increasingly unpopular and it is this factor, more than the attempted assassination attempt by Orsini, that can account for Napoleon's wish to be involved in a successful war against Austria. One overriding factor for Louis Napoleon was the support of French Catholics, which is why his contribution to the cause of Italian unity was limited. In 1859, he was a happy to sign an independent agreement with the Austrians at Villafranca because National Society uprisings in central Italy threatened the Papal States and the temporal power of the papacy.

The issue of Rome after 1861 was to remain a bone of contention between the new Italian state and the French government. In September 1864, an agreement was made between the two powers that the French would withdraw their garrison but the new Italian state would protect Rome from invasion. The latter point was unlikely and, in 1867, Louis Napoleon sent a force to prevent a revolutionary army led by Garibaldi from taking Rome. The defeat of Garibaldi's force at the Battle of Mentana marked the end of a sorry affair for Italian nationalism. It is also another example of how domestic politics dominated Louis Napoleon's decision-making process.

THE ROLE OF PRUSSIA

The role of Prussia in the creation of an Italian nation state should not be underestimated for the simple reason that it was the rising economic and military power of Europe. Throughout 1859, Louis Napoleon had to take into account the attitude of the Prussians to Italian unification. Although the Prussian leadership in 1859 was unsympathetic to the plight of Austria, it also lacked sympathy with the cause of what it saw as revolutionary nationalism. The irony, of course, is that both Cavour and Louis Napoleon were anything but revolutionary – but that was not the point.

On 24 June 1859, the Prussian army mobilised an army on the banks of the Rhine. Fearing that the British government would fail to support him, Napoleon sued for peace with the Austrians at Villafranca. By the terms of the treaty the Austrians would give up Lombardy (but not the Quadrilateral fortresses) to France, but would be able to keep Venice. Although Prussia was not the threat it would be ten years later, mobilisation of its army on the Rhine was enough to push Louis Napoleon into the arms of the Austrians. To the satisfaction of the Austrian emperor, Franz Joseph, the Prussians were made to 'look foolish', but he missed the point. The threat of Prussian intervention was enough to bring Napoleon to the negotiating table.

THE INFLUENCE OF BRITAIN

In *The Struggle for Mastery in Europe 1848–1918* (1954), **A.J.P. Taylor** wrote: 'Italy owed most to French armies and British moral approval.' The coming to power in Britain in June 1859 of the second ministry led by Lord Palmerston had an important impact on the process of unification. Not all British politicians were keen to see the creation of a united Italy, but Palmerston and his highly influential foreign secretary, Lord John Russell, definitely were. Neither politician wished to see the maintenance of Austrian power in northern Italy and both were adamantly opposed to any extension of French interest in the region.

Although the memories of Bonapartist expansion in Italy were, by now, more than 40 years old, they were still fresh enough to influence British foreign policy. The Villafranca agreement of 1859 between France and Austria raised the spectre of a Franco-Austrian *entente* over northern Italy that the British government would not accept. The Crimean War had shown that the balance of power in Europe was shifting. Palmerston and Russell were determined that part of this shifting power did not result in increased foreign domination of the Italian peninsula. The French annexation of Nice and Savoy agreed in March 1860 was bitterly opposed by Palmerston who told D'Azeglio that: '[Napoleon] has vast conceptions [ideas] which he plans to realise and which will force us to make war.'

In the mind of both Palmerston and Russell, the solution to the Italian Question was to support the growth of Piedmontese power. In Turin, the British ambassador Sir James Hudson was to play an important role in the restoration of Cavour as prime minister in January 1860, meeting with Victor Emmanuel a number of times to persuade him that this was in Piedmont's best interests. Britain saw an Italy run as a liberal constitutional monarchy as an important counterbalance to any potential alliance of the conservative monarchies of Austria, Prussia and Russia. As their 1815 settlement crumbled, so Russell in particular was keen to see the creation of a more liberal Europe.

By late-1860, the situation for Russell was critical. He was worried about the possibility of both French and Austrian expansion in Italy. As the armies of Victor Emmanuel were involved in the south in the autumn of 1860, so Russell feared some backlash against events in Italy. In October 1860, the emperors of Austria, Prussia and Russia met at Warsaw. But they failed to come up with a plan to tackle what they considered to be an Italian 'revolution'. Instead, Russia broke diplomatic relations in protest at the unseating of the ruling House of Bourbon in Naples, and Austria reinforced its army in Venetia. However, the three monarchies did not come up with a plan to prevent the unification of the peninsula.

The prospect of conservative action was enough for Russell. On 27 October 1860, he issued a public note that was to have a profound impact on the course of events and, more than any other factor, was to confirm the events of the previous day, when Garibaldi met with Victor Emmanuel at Teano. While Louis Napoleon expressed concern that the papacy was under threat, Russell's pronouncements effectively destroyed the Treaty of Vienna once and for all. He asserted British support for the newly unified Italy because it was the result of the assertion of what

Russell saw as the popular will. Of course, the process of unification had nothing to do with popular will, but this was not the point. Russell praised the idea of 'a people building up the edifice of their liberties'.

In a second note, Russell attacked the despotic rule of the Papal States and the Kingdom of Naples, and clearly warned that if any other power intervened to undermine the new state, then Britain would intervene militarily. But the note was never sent, because Queen Victoria, who was more sympathetic to Austria, has misgivings about its content. However, the support expressed in the first note acted as a guarantee of the new state. Russell's actions should, therefore, be seen as critically important.

THE DECLINE OF AUSTRIA

It can be argued that the slow progress of the cause of nationalism in Italy between 1815 and 1848 was due to the strength and the endurance of Austrian hegemony. The Treaty of Vienna had left the Habsburgs in direct control of Lombardy and Venetia, and Austrian rulers in Tuscany and Modena. The monarchies of the Kingdoms of Sardinia and Naples, and (to a lesser extent) the papacy were restored in the context, and the spirit of Vienna and the nature of their regimes was (to a large) extent, dictated by Vienna. In *The Italian Risorgimento* (1998), **Martin Clark** argues that, 'Even Piedmont, the most "independent" state in Italy, relied ultimately on Austrian force.' As long as that force remained unchallenged, so the political settlement of Vienna would remain unchallenged. At the heart of Prince Metternich's foreign policy was a determination to stamp out any revolution and the preservation of the *status quo*. He also rejected the concept of a liberal constitution and although most restoration states were not especially authoritarian, none granted constitutions.

The demand of most of the revolutionaries in 1821 and 1831 was the granting of greater constitutional liberty, not national unity. But such liberty stood in direct contrast to the wishes of Metternich and Austrian force was used as the means by which such liberty was denied. In April 1821, the Piedmontese revolution collapsed with the defeat of constitutionalist forces at Novara by an Austrian army. Similarly, absolutist rule was restored in Naples after the Troppau Protocol that gave Austria a mandate to intervene.

The British and French had deep reservations about the principle established at Troppau that the great powers had the right to intervene to crush revolution in Europe. However, neither challenged the principle that the political stability of the Italian peninsula was the responsibility of Austria. Although the right of Austria to intervene and crush the revolutions of 1831 was challenged by France, it was Austrian arms that eventually restored order in the Papal States and Austrian troops remained garrisoned in Bologna until 1838. Naturally, there was tension between the papacy and Austria about the extent of Austrian influence in Italy. But the events of 1831 proved that Austrian arms were still the ultimate guarantor of conservative rule in Italy.

While Austria was strong, the stability of the restoration states was assured. By 1848, the diplomatic assumption that it was Austria's prerogative to impose its political views on the Italian states no longer existed. Metternich's reaction to Pius IX's 'liberal' reforms of 1846–7 was to send an army to garrison the town of Ferrara. This move provoked a considerable protest among other rulers on the peninsula and spurred some, including Charles Albert in Piedmont, to further reform.

The fall of Metternich in March 1848 and the financial crisis that followed it were perceived as signs of terminal decline. But Austrian power in Italy was to remain strong for a time after 1848. Although Austrian forces in Italy were decimated by desertion and were forced, in March 1848, to withdraw to the Quadrilateral, they still were far too strong in battle for anything the Piedmontese and their Italian allies could throw at them. The crushing defeats suffered by the Piedmontese at Custozza in July 1848 and Novara in March 1849, as well as the collapse of the Venetian Republic in August 1849, reflected the continuing strength of Austria. However, it was Pius IX's issuing of the Allocution in April 1848 that revealed the reality of power in Italy. Even if Pius wished for the expulsion of Austria from Italy, Austria was too strong to be realistically challenged, even in a year of such turmoil as 1848.

It is without doubt that, ultimately, it was Austrian decline that made political change possible in Italy. That decline was relative to the increasing power of Prussia and the roots of the change in the balance of power were economic. The development from 1819 of a Prussian-dominated free trade system, the Zollverein, gave the north German states involved an economic advantage over Austria. It was one of a number of factors that led to Prussia challenging Austria's leadership of the loose arrangement of states known as the German Confederation.

In the light of events in 1848, the newly crowned Habsburg emperor, Franz Joseph, attempted to reassert control of his empire. One method he used was a policy of Germanisation, introduced by the Minister of the Interior, Alexander Bach. In an attempt to challenge Prussian economic dominance, in 1849 and 1852 the Habsburgs tried to create a southern Germany/middle Europe equivalent of the Zollverein. The attempt failed. Most of the southern German states such as Silesia were already closely bound into the Prussian-dominated economic system. However, the decline of Austrian political power was not apparent in the early 1850s.

An attempt by Prussia to assert its leadership of at least the north of Germany with the creation of a Prussian League in 1850 led to its humiliation, Austria successfully demanding the disbanding of the League by the Treaty of Olmutz in 1850.

Prussia was prepared to back down in the face of Austrian political pressure in 1850 because of the clear superiority of Austrian arms. Just as the Piedmontese had found the Austrian army under Radetzky too powerful in 1848–9, so the Prussians were not in a position to challenge Austrian military supremacy. However, 1850 was the high point of Austrian military hegemony. For the next fourteen years, Prussia consolidated its economic leadership of the Germanic world and by doing so isolated and weakened Austrian power. In 1853, Hanover, Brunswick and Oldenburg joined the Zollverein, thereby completing the economic union of all of non-Austrian dominated Germany. The accession to the Prussian throne in 1861 of Wilhelm I and his appointment of Albert von Roon as Minister of War and Bismarck as Minister-President in 1862 were to have an important effect on Austrian power.

In March 1862, Bismarck agreed a free trade treaty between Prussia and France that excluded Austria. While allied militarily in the period 1862–4, Austria and Prussia duelled for the economic leadership of the German world. Whereas the Prussians preferred the idea of a Prussian-dominated free trading zone, the Austrians preferred a German trading zone that would include all German states and destroy the power of the Zollverein. The Prussians won and, in 1864, German states such as Bavaria, Nassau and Hesse, normally under the dominance of Austria, joined the Zollverein. The military victory of Prussian arms against Austria at Sadowa resulted in the transfer of Venice to Italy via Napoleon. Of course, this was a mere sideshow to the central issue that it confirmed Prussian dominance of Germany and the relative decline of Austria.

THE SIGNIFICANCE OF THE CRIMEAN WAR

In 1866, Italy became a rather lucky beneficiary of the change of the balance of power in Germany, gaining Venice despite heavy defeats at Custozza and Lissa. In reality, this change in the balance of power was further evidence of the collapse of the Vienna Settlement of 1815, which had kept Italian nationalism at bay for so long and had been the foundation of Austrian power in Italy.

The collapse of the system of international agreement was clear after Prussia's defeat of Austria in 1866 in that there was no Congress to discuss the peace; it was dictated by Prussia. The cornerstone of Austrian diplomatic strength from 1815 had been the alliance with other conservative monarchies and their shared desire to keep the forces of revolutionary nationalism at bay. Of particular importance for Austria was its alliance with Russia. However, this alliance collapsed during the Crimean War, which was to prove the watershed for Austrian power. From 1854, Austria and Russia were to become rivals in the Balkans.

In August 1854, Austria, Britain and France issued the **Vienna Four Points**, which effectively ended any possibility of regaining the Austro-Russian alliance in the near future. In December 1854, Austria made a secret treaty with Britain and France in which it was agreed that Austrian possessions in Italy be guaranteed for the duration of the war. Of course, this would have made impossible any Italian uprising in 1854. But it was an unrealistic course of action for nationalists at this time. Austria also signed an alliance with Prussia in 1854 against any potential Russian aggression. But this treaty also gave little diplomatic security for the future. Austria did not join the war against Russia because Russian armies evacuated the regions around the Danube that they had occupied in May 1853. However, it was on the winning side and took its place, alongside Cavour, at the Paris Peace treaty negotiations in 1856.

One should not underestimate the significance of the diplomatic impact of the Crimean War for the cause of Italian unification.

- Austria was now effectively isolated diplomatically. It had lost its great ally, Russia, and was forced to ally with an ultimately unreliable Prussia.
- Neither France nor Britain would, in the medium term, prove to be sympathetic to maintaining Austrian power in northern Italy and its dominant position over the whole peninsula.

The diplomatic consequences of the Crimean War had an important impact on political change in Italy. In many ways, 1856 was the critical diplomatic turning point.

CONCLUSION

The destruction of the Vienna Settlement and the relative decline in the power of Austria were to prove critical factors in facilitating political change in Italy. The undermining of the Europe of Metternich and the assertion of Prussian military and economic power were intertwined. The interest of France and, in particular, the intervention of French armies were necessary as the means by which Austrian domination could be challenged. The diplomatic pressure of Britain and the interest of Palmerston and Russell were to prove essential, especially given Britain's diplomatic importance at the time.

SECTION 5

What were the significant economic, social and cultural divisions in Italy in the period 1848–71?

KEY POINTS

- The period in question saw slow industrial growth and little change in the traditional forms of agriculture.
- The fundamental division was between the north and south. This division was made worse rather than healed by political unification in 1861.
- Cultural divisions were considerable, but the lack of an Italian consciousness should not be exaggerated – especially among the literate classes.

ECONOMIC GROWTH

Research about Italian economic history, especially the volume of imports and exports before unification, is hampered by the lack of evidence. In *The Growth of the Italian Economy 1820–1960* (2001), **Jon Cohen** and **Giovanni Federico** point out that there are few reliable figures about the economy pre-1861 because:

- some states did not collect the appropriate detail
- others such as Lombardy were part of the Austrian Empire
- there was a considerable amount of smuggling.

In 1848, agriculture dominated the economies of the Italian states. Because of the poverty of data there is considerable debate as to whether agricultural production grew in the period in question. The general consensus seems to be that production rose in line with the population increase, but that there was little or no capital investment in agricultural improvement. The dominant crops were wheat and other cereals, which were used as the basic source of food. Other important crops were silk and grapes. By 1870, almost 2 million hectares was under vine cultivation.

LAND

The issue of land ownership was the foremost issue of the day. In *The Italian Risorgimento* (1998), **Martin Clark** asserts that, throughout the nineteenth century, 'the real political issue was not constitutional liberty, nor independence, nor unification, but land'. As opportunities for investment in industry were so weak for much of the period in question, so land was the main form of investment.

The period of Napoleonic rule had seen the abolition of feudal laws and the sale of Church land, which further encouraged land speculation. However, this did not result in a significant broadening of the range of people who owned land. In Piedmont there was more of a tradition of peasant landownership than elsewhere on the peninsula. In the middle of the century there were around 800,000 estates in Piedmont, although it should be stressed that many of these were small. There was a significant difference in the patterns of land cultivation between the north and south. The soil in the south was inferior in quality and the region was crippled by malaria. Land was owned by absentee landlords and rented out by peasant farmers under a system known as the *latifundia*. Throughout Italy and especially in the south, many were landless forced to work as labourers, but suffering from chronic underemployment.

Throughout the nineteenth century, changes to land ownership and how the land was exploited made matters considerably worse for the landless. Many depended on common land for fuel and food. In the 1830s, this land was sold off by local councils, enclosed and common rights lost. By the mid-1860s, about a quarter of a million acres had been sold. The critical issue was who would benefit from the sale of common land? Not surprisingly, it was sold to those close to the local prefects, councillors and mayors. Once they had assumed ownership of this land they exploited it. The increasing demand for wood in the 1840s, in particular from the railway and shipbuilding industries, led to widespread deforestation. As a result, landslides and the erosion of topsoil led to the creation of swamps, which made the malaria worse. It is little wonder that peasants in the south were in a constant state of unrest. This was to work to the advantage of the architects of Italian unification.

In 1860, Garibaldi's invasion of Sicily was preceded by a peasant uprising, which did much to convince the ruling Bourbons that they should flee. At first, Garibaldi issued decrees – including the promise of land – that pleased the peasantry. However, he was forced to go back on his promise, and eventually side with the Sicilian landowners and middle class against the peasantry. Land redistribution in Italy in the mid-nineteenth century was deemed less revolutionary than the political upheaval of the *Risorgimento*.

There was little significant peasant support for the *Risorgimento* from the peasantry because often those who called for insurrection were seen as more of an opponent than the old regime. In 1848, the revolutions were mainly urban based in Milan, Rome, Venice, Florence and Turin. The support for these revolutions was drawn from the artisan class. In Sicily, the peasantry invaded the common lands and demanded their restoration. However, they were quickly thrown off the land and the new Sicilian Parliament failed to pass any land reform measures. One reason why the peasantry failed to respond to the call for national unity is that it was based on a Mazzinian idealism that did not go so far as to address the issue of land. Most land was worked on the basis of subsistence farming with little capital available and primitive farming techniques.

The division between landowner and the middle class on the one hand and the peasant and landless on the other did not improve after 1861. The unification of Italy heralded the sale of large tracts of Church land. In 1867, an Act was passed that began the nationalisation of Church land. In the next nine years, around half a million acres were sold. In the north, peasant farmers bought land. However, in central and southern Italy it was a different story. Land was mainly bought by the middle classes and those who had capital. Those peasants who bought land often found they could not afford the interest payments on the money they borrowed. Additionally, they had little or no capital with which to improve the land and were therefore forced to sell what they had recently acquired.

The process of political unification was not accompanied by significant land reform. But this was little surprise, because those who shaped the political change did so in part to avoid social change. Cavour recognised that:

> *In Italy a democratic revolution has little chance of success. The party* [those wishing for change] *meets with little sympathy among the masses which, except for one or two sections in the towns, are generally attached to the old institutions of the country.*

INDUSTRIAL DEVELOPMENT

In no sense could Italy be described as being industrialised by 1860. It's true, there were signs of industrial development in certain regions, but the base of this development was narrow, being almost exclusively focused in textiles and light industry. There were a number of factors that hindered economic development in Italy and made any development there uneven.

- The Apennines, which form the physical spine of the country, acted as a barrier to transport communication between east and the west of the country.
- The political divisions made for localised rather than nationally based economies.
- The Restoration of 1815 reinforced this localism and generally had a negative effect on industry.
- Tariffs were re-imposed on trade between Italian states.
- Many regions suffered from economic depression.

However, the period after 1815 saw the beginning of industrial growth. Most importantly, machines were imported from (primarily) Britain, France and Switzerland, which led to the creation of a factory-based textile industry. (In 1810, for example, the entrepreneur John Muller imported the machinery necessary for cotton manufacture.) However, there were factors that limited industrial growth, not least of which was that Italy relied on Britain for coal imports. Therefore, although cotton, wool and silk industries grew steadily, in 1844 there were only 114,000 industrial workers in Piedmont.

There was no sense in which the regions of northern Italy were integrated industrially. Indeed, because of Austrian domination of Lombardy and Venetia the region's industries were in direct competition with those of its neighbours. The Lombard cotton industry was the more advanced because Lombard entrepreneurs running businesses (such as Turati) organised their industry in ways that lowered the cost of importing raw cotton. But at least the Piedmontese did not suffer from the impact of protectionism that hampered the industrial growth of their Lombard and Venetian neighbours. There is little doubt that Habsburg red tape restricted industrial growth in Lombardy. It is also clear that, in Lombardy, the industrial economy was not broad enough to avoid severe depression. Rather, it was concentrated in a number of urban centres such as Milan with the effect that when there was a depression, the impact on the industrial regions was considerable.

Silk was the most important industry in Lombardy. But even by the middle of the century there were only around 4400 silk looms, which were based primarily in Como and Milan. When depression struck in 1847, there was widespread suffering. It is likely that industrial growth was only very gradual. Gross Domestic Product (GDP) per head rose in northern and central Italy by only around 0.5 per cent a year between 1830–60. Even by 1871, the extent of an industrialised economy was limited, with just over 15,000 'workshops' – a term that could include factories. Industry was still very much based at home and mostly linked to agricultural production.

If industrial growth was slow in the north, it was virtually non-existent in the south. In *Italy in the Age of the Risorgimento 1790–1870* (1983), **Harry Hearder** suggests: 'Little needs to be said about industry in the Kingdom of Naples because there was little.' Railways had been built in and around Naples in the 1830s, as is explained below. Additionally, there were some industrial enterprises in the city – mainly metal and textile based. But the south suffered from a number of factors that hindered its development. There were few entrepreneurs with skills or capital to invest and few skilled workers. Also, industry was artisan-based in small workshops rather than factories, for the simple reason there was little natural source of power with which to run machinery. Despite these problems, silk and other textiles industries were protected by a system of high tariffs and relatively low taxation. This protection was removed in 1861 with the destruction of internal tariff barriers and the introduction of higher taxes by a new Italian state desperate to clear the debt accumulated in the wars of the *Risorgimento*.

THE RAILWAYS

At the heart of industrial change across Europe (including Italy) was the railway network. For a short period in the 1830s, the Kingdom of Naples had led the way. Indeed, the first railway built on the Italian peninsula was the line completed on 3 October 1839, linking Naples to the nearby suburb of Portici. The stretch of track was the first section of the Naples–Nocera–Castellammare line, and its construction (called *Vesuviana*) stimulated the local engineering industry. Although the first locomotive used on the line was built in Naples from parts made in Britain, an engineering factory was set up for the construction of locomotives at Pietrarsa. But one should not exaggerate the extent of such an initiative. Whereas the city of Naples was connected to suburban districts by the railways, in 1860 over five-sixths of villages in the Kingdom of Naples did not have proper roads, being connected instead by a series of tracks. Despite the fact that the first railway was built in the south, construction was not sustained and in 1860 there were only around 160 kilometres of operating railway track.

Thus, in 1860 the state of the Italian transport system was still extremely poor. Whereas in Britain, canal and rail construction and improvement had formed the basis of an integrated transport system, this was most definitely not the case in Italy. Despite the attempt of Cavour to encourage the construction of canals in Piedmont, generally there was little interest in promoting this important form of industrial transport because of Italy's topography and the lack of excess water. Ironically, it was the regions under the rule of foreign powers that led the way. In Lombardy, in 1819, the canal linking Milan to Pavia opened.

Additionally, Milan was linked to a number of European cities by stagecoach. A few railways were built across the north Italian plains, and in 1857 the Venetian and Lombard railway systems were linked together. It is clear that the poverty of transport in the south acted as a break on agricultural and industrial development. In the southern region of Apulia, for example, the development of an emerging olive oil industry was stunted by the lack of any modern transport system.

However, in 1860 a national transport system became not just an economic priority but a political necessity. In *The Economic History of Modern Italy* (1964), **S.B. Clough** describes how, after political unification, there was 'an almost frantic effort on the part of the government to get the railways built where they did not exist'. Such an enterprise was expensive, especially given the fact that most of the raw materials had to be imported.

In 1865, the railways were transferred into private hands, but the state was still forced to provide a significant amount of capital. In the 1870s, for example, it invested 140 million lire in railway construction. A national system that would allow trade to develop and would unite the disparate provinces of the country was a political priority. The effect of building the railways was considerable on the economy and Italian society. When the Mont Cenis tunnel through the Alps was completed by 1871, the Italian railway network was linked to that in France. This was of utmost importance, given the benefits of increased volume of trade between the two countries. It led to the development of engineering, iron and steel industries. But these industries were based primarily in the north, and in that sense the railways helped to encourage the development of a dual economy rather than a unified one.

It has been argued by **E. Serini** in *Capitalism and the National Market* (1966) that the building of the railways had an important effect in that it stimulated the demand for factory-made goods, because they could be transported around the country more easily. However, the impact of railway building as a whole in Italy was not as great as in the other leading industrial nations of the period. By 1913, Italy still had only half the mileage of railway per head of Britain and France.

CULTURAL DIVISIONS

In *Italy: A Modern History* (1959), **Denis Mack-Smith** made the point of revealing that both Garibaldi and Cavour had 'an imperfect knowledge of the Italian language'. The latter, in particular, preferred to converse in French. At first it seems ironic that two of the leading characters of the story of Italian unification were not fluent in Italian. However, there was no native Italian tongue. The Italian peninsula was a patchwork of languages and regional dialects. The Italian language as we know it came from the Tuscan dialect and was only spoken in Florence. Indeed in 1871, it is likely that it was only known and commonly used by around 630,000 of Victor Emmanuel's new subjects out of a population of nearly 27 million. This lack of linguistic understanding was compounded by an illiteracy rate in 1871 of around two-thirds of the population (literacy being measured by the relatively straightforward task of signing one's name and reading a brief piece of text). It is assumed that such cultural diversity was at the heart of Metternich's dismissal of Italy as a 'mere geographical expression' in 1815 and D'Azeglio's concern that the first priority of the rulers of the new state in 1861 was to 'make Italians'.

The claims that Italy was linguistically and culturally hopelessly divided are a touch simplistic. In the late 1830s and 1840s, a number of national institutions emerged such as the *Congresso degli Scienziata*, which used Tuscan Italian as the common tongue. This was also the common written language which, while accessible only to the literate, became more widely used as the nineteenth century developed. The language of Dante was the recognised language of the educated classes. It was popularised in the widely read second edition of the novel *I Promessi Sposi*, published between 1840 and 1842 and written by Alessandro Massoni. Other writers including D'Azeglio also wrote in Italian rather than French, which was the conversational language of the upper class. Even more important than literature to the sense of cultural unity of the class that could access the culture was opera. The most outstanding composer of the period was Giuseppe Verdi. His works were performed not just in his native Parma but across Italy, again pointing to the concept of a shared culture.

However, this cultural unity occurred only at a certain social level and was limited to the educated and literate. Against it should be weighed the deep chasms of social and cultural division that were experienced throughout the nineteenth century. It is difficult to generalise about the experience of different social classes across the Italian peninsula, as there were so many regional variations. However, the period of Napoleonic rule resulted in a shift in land holding from the old aristocracy to the emerging middle class, especially in the areas in the north such as Lombardy.

One should not exaggerate the extent of the decline of the nobility's economic power. Many nobles benefited from the sale of common land in the 1830s and 1840s, as they did from the sale of Church land in the 1860s. In the 1830s, the old nobility of Lombardy still owned around a third of the cultivated land. However, they were challenged by an emerging middle class that sought to buy land as a means of securing social status.

The relationship between the middle class and the aristocracy has caused some historical debate. In *The Italian Risorgimento* (1998), **Martin Clark** argues that the migration of many aristocrats to urban areas led to a fusion of interests between them and the middle class. To Clark this is a critical point as 'it is the key to understanding the *Risorgimento*. It created an effective new elite, used to acting together and less beholden to the existing states.' This viewpoint is countered in *Italy: A Modern History* (1959) by **Denis Mack-Smith**, who saw the decline in the nobility as leading to friction with the emerging middle class that sought economic and political power. He wrote that 'the *Risorgimento* was a civil war between the old and new ruling class'. Evidence for both can be found, depending on the regions one studies. In Sicily the nobility remained aloof and declined the opportunity to modernise, whereas in Tuscany there was a greater fusion of interest. This often helps explain the nature of the course of the *Risorgimento* in various regions.

The greatest cultural division in Italy was between the wealthier classes and the mass of the poor. For most of those living on the Italian peninsula, the question of the day was not the political shape of Italy or of constitutions but of daily survival. The threat to that survival came from a number of sources. Add to this the diversity of language and culture, and the lack of communication and education, and one can understand why the peasantry and urban workforce were invariably the classes that resisted any political change that might make their plight worse.

The greatest threats to existence were hunger and disease. Across much of the peninsula the peasantry lived on a diet of maize, which had potential implications for health including vitamin deficiency. Cities such as Naples and Palermo were often visited by diseases such as cholera, and the countryside – most obviously the south – was riddled with malaria. The main problem for many was underemployment. As a result there was migration and emigration before 1871 on a wide scale, mainly from the northern provinces. In 1871 alone, more than 120,000 Italians emigrated, most to other parts of Europe but some to America, to find work.

CONCLUSION

The divisions within the Italian peninsula were considerable. The lack of industry, the slow economic growth, and social and cultural division all contributed to a certain economic and social stagnation. Therefore, the dynamic for political change came from above – from a social class that benefited from the sale of cheap land, shared a common means of cultural expression and took part in the economic modernisation that did take place in this period.

SECTION 6

What were the strengths and limitations of a united Italy in 1871 and beyond?

KEY POINTS

- The continuation of the **division** between 'real' Italy and 'legal' Italy is the most obvious evidence of the failure to achieve unification. The political process essentially consisted of making Piedmontisation acceptable to political groupings that stood outside the small Liberal elite. The methods used were a combination of *trasformismo* and concessions.
- There were many groups that lay outside this system, either by choice (for example, the Catholics and Nationalists) or by being rejected (for example, the Councils of Labour). It is more accurate to argue that the Liberal regime did not intend to integrate or unify 'real' Italy into the political system. One need look no further than the restricted suffrage or the widespread use of repression to verify this point.
- There is little evidence of unification becoming the catalyst for economic integration. In fact, one should argue the opposite. The large numbers seeking to emigrate and the absence of any coherent or cohesive social norms or values developing as a consequence of unification reiterate the argument against unification being much more than an imposition of 'legal' Italy, even by 1914.

POLITICAL UNITY

From 1871, the strategy of the liberal establishment was to build broad coalitions in Parliament that could sustain it in power. This was managed through granting political favours and accepting that, at a local level, power would be held by notables as mayors of the '*comuni*'. This acceptance by central government of a certain degree of power was not the same as the decentralisation debated by Cavour and others in 1860. It was an arrangement that benefited those in central government. The agents of the state at a local level, be they mayors or prefects, further strengthened the central state, however, as there was a compatibility of aim: the maintenance of power.

The government of the Italian state revolved around granting favours to deputies to secure a majority and, at election time, granting favours to the electorate to gain the right deputy. Most important, the electorate was

KEY CONCEPT

Division In the words of the Italian writer Gramsci, 'Italy' lacked 'hegemony'. Gramsci was an Italian communist who was imprisoned by the fascists from 1926 to his death in 1937. His writings in prison were prodigious and form a powerful analysis of, among other things, the unification process and the development of Italy post-1871. By arguing that Italy lacked hegemony, he stated that Italy lacked leadership and a shared set of values recognised by all. This stemmed from the narrow social base of those in power that existed in Italy at the time of the unification.

limited and in no sense representative as a whole. In 1870, it was half a million (2.2 per cent of adult men); in 1880, it was 622,000 (8 per cent of adult men). In 1874, the successful candidate in any constituency would receive no more than about 500 votes.

There was a geographically-based electoral divide, even after extended suffrage in the 1880s and 1890s. By 1895, 56 per cent of the electorate was in the north, 26 per cent in the south, and the remainder in the central regions of Italy. The electorate was literate and even subsequent suffrage reforms post-1871 maintained a literacy requirement, as had been dictated in the *Statuto* of 1848. Similarly, the electorate remained predominantly urban.

In the main, such an electorate produced a political class that was receptive to *trasformismo*. The criticism of this system was that those who were 'absorbed' (such as the Radicals who gave support to the 'left' governments of Depretis and Cairoli after 1876) were not representative of 'real' Italy as a whole and were estranged by their absorption. An example of this phenomenon was the low Radical vote in artisan and working-class areas of Milan in 1886. Many deputies from the south were supportive of successive administrations from 1882 onwards, not because those regimes acted in the interest of the south but because of the corrupt nature of Parliamentary politics. To all intents and purposes, the southern elite were bought off as an alternative to political integration.

The process of absorption was undermined by the development of mass politics towards the end of the nineteenth century – especially the socialists and Catholics. Because of its nature, absorption could not accommodate the aspirations of large groups, partly because these groups were less likely to be bought off with piecemeal concessions and partly because acceding to the demands of one group could upset another. It was a political balancing act, but vulnerable at all times as a consequence. An excellent example was during Giovanni Giolitti's period in office as prime minister. The **Gentiloni pact of 1912** and Giolitti's reliance on the Catholics thereafter offended the Radicals, who were steeped in anti-clericalism. Hence they withdrew their support from the government.

THE LIMITS TO THE SYSTEM OF ABSORPTION

The roots of the policy of absorption go back to Cavour's *connubio* of the 1850s. However, as with the *connubio*, the system would always have its weaknesses. The process of political absorption was never fully comprehensive, as the extent to which Giolitti was able to absorb the Socialist movement proves.

From 1900, Giolitti was able to absorb large numbers of socialist deputies with social welfare policies such as the state Maternity Fund of 1910. These deputies (known as 'reformists') were generally middle class, 22 out of 28 deputies in 1904 having a university education. Their class was dictated by the composition of the electorate, and many deputies, such as the PSI leader Filippo Turati, sympathised with the aims of the radicals and the policies of Giolitti. Yet it could never be argued that the liberal regime managed to 'absorb' the socialist movement. Too much of it lay outside the world of parliamentary politics.

An example of this was the General Confederation of Labour (CGL) formed in 1906, and the Chambers of Labour, which acted independently of the main socialist party the PSI. The latter in particular had great influence in certain areas, as could be seen in its control of the labour market in Emelia from 1904. There were socialist co-operatives in the countryside; by 1910 they had 218,000 members.

REPRESSION

The significance for the political system was that, to a greater extent, many of these groups lay outside and in opposition to the establishment – with 200 people dying in strike-related violence between 1900 and 1904. Such violence made full support for the establishment, even by the reformist deputies, impossible.

After 1912, with the rise of the left and the demise of Turati's reformist wing, absorption became even harder to achieve. Strikes and violence led to resentment against the system from employers who believed Giolitti to be too sympathetic to socialism – particularly after the general strikes of 1904, the introduction of National Insurance in 1912 and the victory of the union FIOM in the Turin strikes of 1913.

Similarly, the reliance of Giolitti on Catholic-influenced deputies after 1912 alienated the traditionally anti-clerical radical deputies from his coalition. The system that dominated from 1871 to 1912 was based on the manoeuvrings of an elite, a restricted and literate electorate and patronage. The liberal establishment had no broad popular basis, which can be recognised in the limitations of the Giolittian system.

THE CONTINUING PROBLEMS OF CHURCH AND STATE

It is in the relationship between the Catholic Church and state where the absence of reconciliation between 'legal' and 'real' Italy becomes most apparent.

KEY TERM

The Roman Question revolved around the issue of the status of Rome and the decline in the papacy's temporal power. It was the main sticking point in the dispute between Church and state that lasted from 1871 to 1919.

At the heart of the issue were the problems of the **Roman Question** and the status of the Pope. The institutional anti-clericalism of the state was a result of the influence of the radical movement, but primarily due to the dismissal of the state in the *Syllabus of Errors* of 1864, which was translated into the prohibition of Catholics to vote from 1881. The result was a 'duality of influence' – Catholics organising into national groups such as the *Opera dei Congressi* from 1874 with the explicit aim of countering the influence of the state.

Despite its rejection of national politics, Catholics became heavily involved in local government, partly to counter the growing socialist influence and partly to create a base from which they could exert influence of their own. From the 1890s, local government was fought over by Catholics and Socialists for power and influence. While the Catholics were never formed into an organised conservative party, they were the establishment's bulwark against the rise of socialism. This was given impetus by *Rerum Novarum* in 1891 (see page 121).

The extent of *Opera*'s influence in the 1890s (3982 rural banks, 24 newspapers and 105 periodicals in the north) reflects, conversely, on an absence of state influence. The state retaliated by introducing anti-clerical measures such as Crispi's reforms of 1890, which attempted to limit the role of the Church in social welfare, or Prime Minister Antonio di Rudini's dissolving of all Catholic associations in 1897. Although post-1900 such open antagonism between Church and state no longer existed (mainly because of the socialist threat), the Church was not reconciled to the state. It is correct to point out that by 1909, the rule on non-voting had been partially abandoned and *Opera* dissolved by Pope Pius X in 1905. Similarly, Catholics had increasingly become involved in local and even national politics by 1914. The aims of this were twofold: to diminish the influence of socialism as proposed by priests such as the influential Luigi Sturzo, and to further the cause. The primary example of this was the Gentiloni Pact of 1912 (see page 139), which undermined the Giolittian system.

By 1914, the Catholics had maintained an 'otherness', which underlined the limitations of so-called 'unification'. From the women's *Unione Donne Cattoliche*, to the continued role in welfare, the Catholic Church continued to develop parallel institutions to those of the state. Although the start of the new century saw the beginnings of a *rapprochement* between Church and state, the issues that divided them were based on the legitimacy of the state itself. Therefore, in this sphere it is impossible to describe Italy as unified by 1914 and the problems that had existed at the time of unification still remained.

REPRESSION OF POLITICAL OPPONENTS

The persistent threat of popular disaffection is a common thread that runs through this period, as is the repressive nature of the regime in dealing with that threat. This mainly stemmed from the regime's lack of a popular basis, the consequence often being over-reaction when absorption was not possible. Therefore, outbreaks of unrest that had economic causes often developed into politically motivated action. A clear example of this was the unrest of 1898. What started as rioting against high bread prices in January developed into something far more serious in May because of the shooting of demonstrators by the police and common unrest. The consequence of the Milan insurrection was widespread repression (for example, the socialist leader Turati was imprisoned for twelve years).

The awarding of the Cross of Savoy, Italy's most prestigious military decoration, to General Bava Beccaris for his role in the repression characterises the insecurity of the establishment. Indeed, Beccaris' actions in 1898 had inflamed the situation in Milan. He used cannon and cavalry charges against ordinary citizens. He also encouraged the savage sentences on Socialist and Catholic leaders, many of whom had urged restraint. His decoration by the king was considered a scandal in many quarters. However, such insecurity was not limited to 1898. States of 'siege' were declared ten times between 1861 and 1922, entailing the introduction of martial law. This, perhaps more than any other fact, underlines the fragility of Italian unity and the precarious position of the establishment even more than 30 years after unification. Central government used the police, judiciary and prefects to control the regions. Their usage reveals the extent to which the establishment relied on such levers of power to rule effectively. When, in 1904, the local election at Bassano resulted in a Catholic administration, the prefect dissolved the council.

Prefects were responsible for 'fixing' elections, which often resulted in the election of candidates who would support the *status quo*. In the south this resulted in the majority of deputies supporting the government, despite the government doing little for the south as a region. The police were given wide-ranging powers to act in the interest of the state – an example being a system of internal exile, which was used on over 5000 people at any one time in the 1890s. Further police discretionary powers, a state-controlled judiciary and a jury system based on only 30,000 eligible jurors nationwide reinforced the impression of a centralised and defensive state.

NORTH–SOUTH DIVIDE

The greatest division within the Italian state was the economic chasm between north and south. The contrast between a capitalist north (with its large farms, irrigation, technical improvements) and the feudal south (blighted with malaria and sub-division of land) did not change as a consequence of unification. Malaria had a huge effect on the Italian economy. In many southern areas until 1900, it was the main cause of death in agricultural areas and resulted in low-lying land being uncultivable. It was made worse by soil erosion as a consequence of deforestation and the building of railways. The disease was curtailed from the turn of the century with the distribution of quinine. It should be argued that unification reinforced and accentuated the division.

The sale of Church land after 1861 resulted in the consolidation of the economic and political power of the local elites. It is seen to be the case that this class had also benefited from the decline of the feudal system and the auction of common land. Many peasants who bought plots were often forced to resell as the new state imposed increased land taxes. Therefore, the process of land redistribution reflected the balance of political power and reinforced the the feelings of alienation that manifested itself in, for example, the *fasci* of Sicily.

The general tariff imposed on many imported goods in 1887 is further proof of the close relationship between political and economic elites. In 1886–7, nearly 1 million tonnes of cheap wheat were imported, in the main from America. Those who were hardest hit were large wheat-growing landowners, and the Corn Laws – raising duties from 14 lire per tonne in 1887 to 75 lire per tonne by 1894 – were in the interests of that class. The reciprocal tariffs imposed by France and other European countries after 1887 hit the southern agricultural economy of wine and olives particularly hard (wine production fell by around 25 per cent from 1886 to 1890).

THE AGRICULTURAL REVOLUTION?

The 'agricultural revolution' (based on machinery innovation and capital investment) was limited to the north, in particular around the Po Valley. While wheat production in the north grew by 100 per cent from 1873 to 1913, in the south the amount of land cultivating wheat actually fell by 8 per cent between 1883 and 1913.

The state heavily invested in land reclamation, but again the picture is of northern progress and southern stagnation. Of the 352,000 hectares improved by 1915, only 2300 were in the south. The massive emigration discussed on pages 145–6 was indicative of the imbalance of the state's intervention in the agricultural sector. Its priority in the south was to cultivate and maintain the support of the local elites, hence subsidy and legislation were framed in such a fashion to ensure continuity.

In 1906–7, laws relating to Calabria in the south were passed granting tax concessions on land, monies for construction projects and agricultural credit. These reforms were mainly cosmetic. Any attempt at real reforms – such as Prime Minister Sidney Sonnino's proposed land and social reforms of 1906 to create a literate land-owning peasantry in the south – were opposed with great hostility by the southern establishment and were not implemented. The consequence was geographical economic division and social unrest.

INDUSTRIAL DEVELOPMENT AFTER 1871

The industrial development of Italy from 1871 onwards was heavily influenced by the nature of unification. As in agriculture, the chasm between the industries of north and south was made more pronounced. The south benefited from selective state subsidies, such as the government-sponsored industrial development of Naples in 1904. But this system of subsidy was linked to political patronage. The influence of the government in shaping Italy's industrial development was as great as it was revealing of the interests of the government.

There is no doubt that this period saw spectacular industrial growth, the value of manufactured goods doubling between 1896 to 1908 and the national income rising by 32 per cent between 1895 to 1915. State protection from 1887 provided the environment for growth of particular industries such as iron and steel. The capital needed for such large-scale investment was provided by banks such as the Bank *Commerciale Italiana*, which had close links with successive governments. Most instructive of all was the close relationship between the growth of the steel and shipbuilding industries and state funding.

The steel industry was dominated by the firm Terni and, from 1911, by a cartel dominated by **ILVA**. These companies raised capital from the banks such as Bank *Commerciale*, and heavily relied on state subsidies and state orders for warships, in particular from the building of the *Dandolo* (1876) and *Duilio* (1878). As mentioned on page 135, the state also heavily subsidised the building of the railways, although much of the material to build what was a network of 13,600 kilometres by 1890 came from abroad. From nationalisation of the railways in 1905, the state encouraged the further growth of the engineering industry by placing orders (for example, for 3000 carriages) with Italian companies. The picture of industrialisation, therefore, is characterised by the intervention of both government and banks.

THE IMPACT OF PROTECTION

The tariff might have retarded trade with France until an agreement was made in 1898, but there is also no doubt that it protected industries such as steel and cotton from what might otherwise have been fierce competition – the latter seeing a doubling in the number of spinning frames from 1900 to 1914.

It is wrong to characterise all of Italy's industrial growth in this period as being reliant on state encouragement. The motor industry, led by FIAT of Turin (which employed 6500 people and made 4500 cars in 1914), is a classic example of industry flourishing in the atmosphere of confidence that was prevalent after 1896. The key point here is that Italy's industrial growth was reliant on state intervention and thereby reflected the interests of the state.

Initially, unification was a disaster for the industrial south, as the abolition of internal tariffs saw a collapse in some industries that found they could not compete. (For example, in Calabria there was a fall of around one-third in the number of industrial workers between 1881 and 1901.) The benefits of the emerging steel-ship-banks infrastructure were to be felt primarily in the north – Liguria being the centre of the shipbuilding industry, and Piedmont that of engineering. The productive state capital investment was mainly in the north, such as in the burgeoning hydro-electricity industry. The nature of industrial growth was as artificial and as imposed as political unity. Those areas in the north that were favoured flourished (for example, the Po Valley), but many areas remained backward and impoverished. It was partly the consequential obvious economic gap that made a liberal hegemony impossible.

EMIGRATION

The litmus test of a united Italy is the extent to which the state had managed to 'make Italians' out of a geographically, linguistically and culturally divided population in 1871. It should be argued that, as with the political and economic structures, there had developed certain national institutions yet there was no social hegemony and social division predominated. The most obvious manifestation of this fact was the growth of emigration from Italy in the period.

The issue of migration needs to be considered in the wider context of population movement in the period in question. It was not just Italians who migrated; the 'pull' of the United States and the growth of empire meant that large numbers of Europeans, on average 900,000 a year between 1881 and 1915, left their homelands in search of a better future abroad. It should also be pointed out that between 1876 and 1901 the rate of emigration to non-European countries from Ireland and Norway was greater than from Italy.

However, this was not the case after 1900 when the rate of emigration from Italy jumped from 396 emigrants per year per 100,000 of the population in the period 1876–80 to 1938 per year per 100,000 in the period 1906–10. The significance of this figure should not be ignored. It reflects not just the failure to 'make Italians' as pointed out by d'Annunzio but is a direct consequence of state economic policy with regards to both investment and protectionism. The development of Italian society was dysfunctional and emigration is the evidence of the extent of the alienation of swathes of Italians. Although many emigrants were to return, it was the permanent departure of 1.5 million Italians during the period 1900 to 1914 that is so striking.

LINGUISTICS AND LITERACY

A major obstacle to 'making Italians' continued to be the linguistic differences of the peninsula. The widespread lack of knowledge of Italian continued as the Italian state lacked the will and resources to promote widespread education reform. Therefore, improvements in literacy, which would have familiarised Italians with their new mother tongue, remained slow. Yet, to an extent, this was intentional. As has been seen, the illiterate were deliberately excluded from the political process by the restricted suffrage. In reality, this effectively excluded vast swathes of the population of the south.

It is likely that around 70 per cent of the population were illiterate in 1871, a figure that had fallen to just under 40 per cent by 1911. In the province of Calabria, however, illiteracy remained at around 70 per cent of the population in 1911, while in Piedmont it had fallen to 11 per cent! To explain this astonishing difference, one has to look no further than the state of primary education in Italy. Despite supposed compulsory schooling for three years from 1882, the effect of the diet of nationalism fed to students in these schools was mitigated by poor attendance rates. In the 1880s, in the south it was calculated to be as low as 20 per cent – and seasonal at that.

It is true that the state attempted to influence primary education to combat the influence of Catholicism, such as the Daneo-Credaro Law of 1911, which set up Schools Councils, with some government control, to run the primary sector. However, it did not attempt to strengthen primary education throughout Italy. While some northern provinces received 568,000 lire state funding for school building between 1861 and 1911, some areas of Calabria got nothing. In terms of secondary education, the majority of the nation's technical schools and 'popular universities' (secondary education courses set up by universities) were situated in the north. This pattern of education fits in well with the developing economic structure with its accentuated north–south split.

The making of Italians linguistically was a tall order in an age of just-emerging mass communication. In fact, the use of dialect prevailed until after the Second World War and was only broken down by the showing of popular Hollywood movies, which had been dubbed into Italian. The Italian cinema emerged in the 1900s with many films celebrating the glories of unification. By 1914, however, it had not yet quite become the mass entertainment it was to be post-1918. The press also emerged in this period and weeklies such as *Gazzetta dello Sport* (founded in 1896) had a circulation of 1.5 million by the turn of the century.

When the literacy rates are taken into account, though, it is difficult to accept this as an indication of developing national unity. As a whole, the press was not populist but a mirror of the political attitudes of the establishment. Although newspapers such as the influential *Corriere della Sera* criticised the Giolittian system, it was from the standpoint that the system was too introvert. There is no doubt that newspapers such as *Giornale d'Italia* (set up in 1902) were sold nationwide. Yet, again, it is misleading to deduce that this was of a significance in terms of unifying the country culturally. In the south the readership was limited to the elite – those groups that had been absorbed.

THE RISE OF NATIONALISM

The failure of the liberal establishment to unify Italy was reflected in the emergence of a hostile nationalism towards the end of the period. This nationalism should be seen as a critique of the state's failure to build a nation as defined in late nineteenth-century terms. The failure of colonial policy as represented by defeat at Adowa was keenly felt by writers such as Alfredo Rocco and Enrico Corradini, who became the Nationalists' foremost writers.

The main criticism of the Giolittian system and the Liberal state was that it had not followed a foreign policy that represented the nation's interests. Italy's lack of colonies was acutely felt and the defeat in 1896 even more of a national humiliation. The invasion and defeat of Abyssinia should be seen in this light, although Giolitti, being who he was, also invaded Libya to please the Catholic lobby. Yet invading Libya was a crucial error in that it legitimised the mainly extra Parliamentary nationalist movement and destroyed the fragile balance of the compromised political parties. Even through a foreign policy that was generally successful in the security of the Triple Alliance from 1882 and a colonial policy that made some gains despite Adowa, the liberal regime failed to unite Italians into any sense of national purpose.

CONCLUSION

The unification of 1871 was a unification of legal institutions. The political classes that administered this 'legal' Italy attempted to reconcile strategically important groups to the state through a policy of concessions. It repressed those groups that it could not 'absorb' into the system. As time passed, so more groups became 'absorbed'. Yet the policy was never comprehensive and became contradictory. Both social and economic developments reflect the political priorities and necessities of the new state's elites.

That these priorities were often at variance with the interests of swathes of the country's populace was not important, as long as control was maintained by the state apparatus and local elites. That this system eventually crashed is due to its desire to maintain a *status quo* that did not include a politicised population. There were cultural changes over the years between 1871 and 1914, which meant the spread of spoken Italian. In precious few contexts, however, is it possible to talk of a unified Italy by 1914.

A2 ASSESSMENT

INTRODUCTION

The following section should be used by those studying AQA Module 4 Section B. It hopes to give clear advice as to appropriate technique to be used in answering questions.

ESSAY-BASED QUESTIONS IN THE STYLE OF AQA

Candidates taking A2 Option D Module 4 have the choice of answering an essay question on the Italian Unification, 1848–71. There are a number of examples of the type of question you might face. The two issues you need to address are as follows.

- Your essay technique, which will enable you to receive the top marks for your essay.
- The content to be used to answer the question.

You should be clear that you need to look at each question not only in the light of the obvious detail it asks you to use, but also in the wider context. For each of the examples below, the narrow detail and the wider context have been explained.

Example 1

> To what extent was Cavour the 'architect of Italian unification'?

Indicative content. To reach the highest level in this essay, you have to weigh up the relative importance of Cavour against other factors in explaining Italian unification. You also need to deal with the debate about the significance of the role of the individual in relation to other factors. When dealing with Cavour you must identify the extent of his nationalist ambitions – his contribution to the development of the status of Piedmont as well as his diplomatic achievements. These achievements must, of course, be placed in the context of events and the diplomatic objectives of others.

Example 2

> 'The fact that Italy was not unified under the control of the papacy was in the main due to the actions of Pius IX.' How far do you agree with this statement?

Indicative content. In answering this question you should look at the actions of Pius IX, his political aims and the challenges to Church power in the mid-nineteenth century. You should look at the impact of Gioberti, neo-Guelphism and the role played by Cardinal Antonelli. The broader context should be explained in terms of the decline in the Church's temporal power, the change in emphasis to spiritual leadership and increasing identification of nationalism with anti-clericalism.

Example 3

> To what extent do you agree with the claim that 'By 1871 Italy was united in name only'?

Indicative content. To answer this question you need to look at the name of unification, how it occurred as Piedmontisation and how the new centralised political structure was imposed on the regions of Italy in 1861. The question asks you to look at the political divisions that remained by 1871, most obviously the Church but also between the Piedmontese establishment and those who lay outside the political system. You also need to look at the broader context of economic, cultural and social divisions explaining why they were maintained.

ESSAY TECHNIQUE

Essay writing in your Unit 4 examination requires you to show that you can do the following.

- Answer with a sustained judgement throughout the essay.
- Show an understanding of different interpretations.
- Use a broad range of accurate and well-deployed information to back up your answers.
- Place your understanding in the context of broader factors.

Below is a suggested structure for such an essay that will help you reach the top Level 5 in the examination. The main features you need to concentrate on are:

- timing
- the question
- planning
- structure
- directness
- evidence.

Timing. It is essential that you spend exactly the correct amount of time on the essay. To over-write on the essay will not give you any extra marks, but to under-write will lose you marks. You have 45 minutes for each essay. This includes a couple of minutes' reading time at the end, which is absolutely crucial. When you read through your essay, you will then have time to complete, amend and add to it. Examiners can become exasperated with students who have been sloppy.

The question. The most common type of question you will meet demands answers such as 'up to a point, but . . .' and 'to a certain extent, but . . .'. Examples of this type of question include the following.

- How far do you agree . . . ?
- To what extent . . . ?

Planning. This is the key to success. In the plan you directly answer the question, using the words in the question. You have three to four minutes to plan your essay. On no account should your plan be longer than three or four minutes; you do not get marks for your plan.

The purpose behind the plan is for you to work out in your mind the argument in response to the question. You should be aiming in your answer for a mark of 20. To achieve that, you need to be direct in your plan.

- The plan should take the form of three lines/strands of argument. The first two should be the main points, the last a however/but point that makes your argument more sophisticated or complex.
- You then should very briefly highlight what you are going to put in each paragraph. The emphasis here is on brevity – that is, one or two words a paragraph.
- Use your plan as a sketch. You should not complete your plan and then abandon it. Complete your plan and refer to it at all times.

One cannot stress enough the importance of the plan. It is a very important factor in your success.

Below is an example from Question 1: To what extent was Cavour the 'architect of Italian unification'?

- Cavour was the architect to a certain extent in that he played an important role in the modernisation of Piedmont and involving foreign powers in the unification process.
- However his significance should not be exaggerated. He was often a hostage to events and factors beyond his control.
- As significant as Cavour were a number of other individuals and the change in diplomatic circumstances that made unification possible.

Introduction. Once you have written a plan, you need to write an introduction that answers the question. The introduction will involve writing out the main points from the plan. It is essential that you attack the question directly in the introduction. Below is an example of an introduction in response to Question 2: 'The fact that Italy was not unified under the control of the papacy was in the main due to the actions of Pius IX.' How far do you agree with this statement?

The introduction is simple, straightforward, direct and delivers and answer to the question.

To a considerable extent the failure of Pius IX to provide leadership to the nationalist movement, his inherent conservatism and political naivety explain why Italy was not unified under the leadership of the papacy. However, it is too simplistic simply to focus on the role of Pius; the changing focus of the Church, the attitudes of foreign powers and the rise of a nationalism based partly on anti-clericalism are also important factors. Most important was the incompatibility of nationalism with the clericalism of the Church in the nineteenth century.

Paragraph structure. Now we come to the most important part of the essay – the main paragraphs. You need to write paragraphs of a fair length, up to or around two-thirds of a side is a good length paragraph. To achieve the mark you want you need to stay direct to the argument throughout. This means that you explicitly answer the question throughout the essay. The best structure for every paragraph is as follows

- Argue. At the start of the paragraph you should present a line of argument. The best way to do this is to use the language of argument, for example:

One should argue that …
It is clear that …
Fundamentally, …
Without doubt …
This most obviously ….

- Explain. The next sentence or two in the question will explain that line of argument.
- Evidence. *The clearest example of this point is the …* The next section of the paragraph should give and explain the relevance of detail that you have used to back up your argument. This detail needs to be accurate, well selected and relevant. What is meant by detail? Facts, statistics, names, events. Within this evidence you should also pay attention to the views of historians where appropriate. These views should be mentioned, the historians quoted if applicable and the viewpoint discussed. However, on no account should you fall into the trap of simply recounting what a certain historian has said without making it relevant to your line of argument.
- Reiterate. The last half sentence of the paragraph should be a reiteration, going back to the main theme/argument in the question.

Below is an example of a paragraph from an answer to Question 3 (To what extent do you agree with the claim that 'By 1871 Italy was united in name only'?), which attempts to follow this model.

It is clear that the division between Church and state over the issue of the status of Rome and the temporal power of the Church was highly significant. Indeed, given Pius IX's rejection of any compromise with the state in 1871 and given the power and influence of the Church, it is valid to argue that the state was very much weakened by papal opposition. The Church maintained its social status and political influence despite loss of land and anti-clerical legislation throughout the 1860s. Clearly, the most significant issue was that of Rome, as was reflected in the state's generous offer in the Law of Guarantees of 1871 and Pius IX's rejection of the offer. However, at the heart of the division was the Church's rejection of the values embodied by the state in the Syllabus of Errors *of 1864. The introduction of papal infallibility in 1870 reinforced the Church's decision to stand apart from the state and to retreat into spiritual matters. But the state of permanent 'fractious cohabitation' (Martin Clark) was to undermine the new political structure as it removed the possibility of a broad-based conservative party developing in support of the new leaders of Italy. So, the division between Church and state very much support the view that unity in 1871 was only nominal.*

The next paragraph. It is good technique sometimes to explicitly link the paragraphs together. You should try to avoid using the same prefix to open every paragraph as it can become too repetitive.

The 'However …'/'But …' paragraph. The mark schemes insist that you place the factors you have discussed and argued about into a broader context. For you to make your argument more complex you need, perhaps, to qualify or make your argument a touch more complex or sophisticated. This can be done in a number of ways.

- In an 'up to a point … but' answer, you need to look at the 'but' point.
- Often there is a point of qualification to make to your argument – for example, 'However, one should not exaggerate the impact of …'.
- You should try to be explicit about putting your ideas into context. This is an example of the start of a 'However …'/'But …' paragraph from an answer to Question 1.

However, the significance of Cavour can only be fully understood in the context of the changing balance of power in Europe. Most significantly, the relative decline of Austria and the rise of France created the opportunity in which Cavour's diplomatic initiatives could be effective.

Conclusion. Every essay must have a conclusion. However, as with the introduction, it should be very short and to the point.

Style. The structure for each paragraph is the means by which you can write directly to the question. However, I would like to stress again, it is essential that you are explicit in your directness.

SELECTED BIBLIOGRAPHY

The following books are recommended for further reading.

D. Beales and E. Biagini, *The Risorgimento and the Unification of Italy* (Longman, 2002)
M. Clark, *Modern Italy 1871–1995* (Longman, 1996)
M. Clark, *The Italian Risorgimento* (Longman, 1998)
J. Cohen and G. Federico, *The Growth of the Italian Economy 1820–1960* (Cambridge UP, 2001)
J. Davis and P. Ginsborg, *Society and Politics in the Age of the Risorgimento* (Cambridge UP, 2002)
C. Duggan, *A Concise History of Italy* (Cambridge UP, 1994)
J. Gooch, *The Unification of Italy* (Methuen, 1986)
H. Hearder, *Italy in the Age of the Risorgimento 1790–1870* (Longman, 1983)
H. Hearder, *Cavour* (Longman, 1984)
E. Holt, *Risorgimento: the Making of Italy 1815–70* (MacMillan, 1970)
D. Mack-Smith, *Victor Emmanuel, Cavour and the Risorgimento* (Oxford UP, 1971)
D. Mack-Smith, *Cavour* (Methuen, 1985)
D. Mack-Smith, *Italy and its Monarchy* (Yale UP, 1994)
D. Mack-Smith, *Mazzini* (Yale UP, 1994)
D. Mack-Smith, *Modern Italy: A Political History* (Yale UP, 1997)
A. Ramm, *The Risorgimento* (The Historical Association, 1962)
A. Sked, *Decline and Fall of the Habsburg Empire 1815–1918* (Longman, 1989)
A. Stiles, *Unification of Italy 1815–70* (Edward Arnold, 1986)
A.J.P. Taylor, *The Struggle for Mastery in Europe 1848–1918* (Clarendon Press, 1954)

INDEX